# 401
# AMAZING ANIMAL FACTS

## Marianne Taylor

Are you going to lie around
photosynthesising all day?

Yes.

NH
NEW
HOLLAND

First published in 2010 by New Holland Publishers
London • Cape Town • Sydney • Auckland
www.newhollandpublishers.com

Garfield House, 86-88 Edgware Road, London W2 2EA, United Kingdom
80 McKenzie Street, Cape Town, 8001, South Africa
Unit 1, 66 Gibbes Street, Chatswood, NSW 2067, Australia
218 Lake Road, Northcote, Auckland, New Zealand

2 4 6 8 10 9 7 5 3 1

*A CIP catalogue record for this book is available from the British Library.*

ISBN 978 1 84773 715 1

Publisher: Simon Papps
Editor: Elaine Rose
Design: Nicola Liddiard
Production: Melanie Dowland

Reproduction in Sigapore by Pica Digital (Pte) LTd
Printed and bound in India by Replika Press Pvt Ltd

...eat the tree, don't eat the tree, eat the tree, don't eat the tree...

## Dedication

*For Graham T, the annoying little brother I never had
and the weirdest animal I've ever met.*

## Acknowledgements

First of all I must thank Graham Taylor, who first suggested
I should write a book of weird animal facts – good thinking,
G-man! I would like to thank Simon Papps at New Holland for
backing this project with such enthusiasm and putting up with
my periodic changes of direction during the writing process.
Elaine Rose did a great job copyediting the text and I was
delighted with Nicki Liddiard's lively design.

Many friends made suggestions for particular facts I should cover,
and I even listened to some of them. Other friends helped just as
much by putting up with me waffling on incessantly about weird
animals for months, so thanks to Michele, Michelle, Graham x2,
Saj, Steve x3, Mike, Imogen and everyone else who let me bend
their ears during the difficult planning stages.

My dad was, as ever, full of useful advice and much-appreciated
encouragement during the writing process, and my cat Pickle
provided constant daily inspiration by being unfailingly weird
in everything she did.

Finally, thanks to Rob for too many reasons to list; the one I
particularly want to highlight is that he came up with far and
away the best cartoon idea in the whole book. Rob, you're a
genius (and I've said it in print now so there's no denying it).

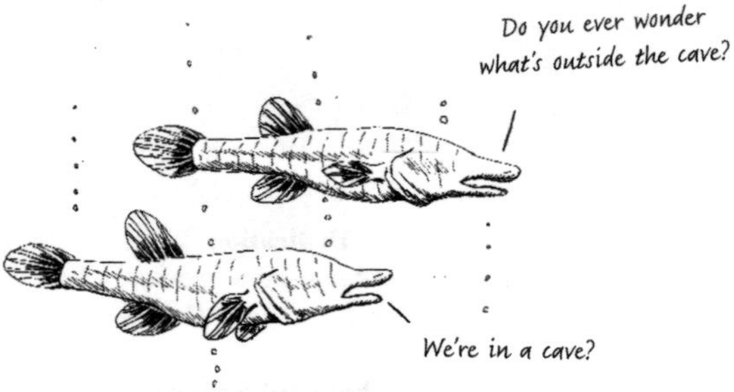
Do you ever wonder what's outside the cave?
We're in a cave?

# CONTENTS

# INTRODUCTION

Aren't animals amazing? You only have to look at the
TV schedule to see that we're as interested in wildlife
as we are in gardening, interior design and holidays in
sunny countries. In our real lives though, most of us don't
have much to do with wild animals; they are pushed to the
margins of our consciousness. Although we (mostly) know
it's true, we don't like to acknowledge that we are a single
shoot of the tree of animal life – that *Homo sapiens* is no
more inherently special or important than any other
animal species.

It's very easy for us westernized humans, installed in
our everything-proof homes, to see the natural world as an
irrelevance. Yet many of the wonderful inventions that

*Ow!*

have enabled us to manipulate our environment so effectively have already evolved in other, often disparate branches of that animal tree, and many of the strangely human behaviours we indulge in have been a part of animal life for an eternity.

We have yet to develop a material as tough and yet as lightweight as spider silk. Bats and dolphins have been using echolocation to find their way around long before we invented sonar. We have sat-nav but migrating birds can find their way by feeling the Earth's magnetic field. We herd cows and grow arable crops; ants herd aphids and grow fungal cultures for food. Individual humans have achieved astounding feats of endurance, but whatever the environment and the challenge, it's a safe bet that there's at least one species of animal that does the same thing every day, only better, faster, longer and with far more style. While no one could really argue that humans are more accomplished than any other species across the board, we'd be kidding ourselves that we have all the best ideas, break all the records and trump every other species on Earth.

He said he felt all shagged out, and then....

*BLEEEAARGH!*

So much for what we have in common with other animals. Look a little further and a little closer and you'll find animals with body shapes, behaviours and abilities that are way beyond anything that makes sense to us. Palaeontologists have dug up fossilized 505-million-year-old animals that are put together in ways which make the best efforts of our sci-fi writers seem blandly unimaginative. There are animals on land and in the sea which can see vast swathes of the electromagnetic spectrum that will forever be invisible to us. Some animals live out their lives under conditions which we could not endure for a second, no matter how much sophisticated safety gear we wear. Animal family life goes to extremes that we find unthinkable – sometimes for its barbarity, sometimes for the astounding degree of self-sacrifice that is made.

This book is a celebration of all that is extraordinary in the animal world. Starting with evolution and ending with animal associations with humans, the chapters explore animal physiology, sensory abilities, migratory journeys, powers of endurance, everything to do with courtship and reproduction, eating habits and social life. From familiar and everyday birds and mammals to the decidedly less well-known velvet worms, mantis shrimps, tunicates and tardigrades, the wild, wide and weird world of animal oddities is here to enthral, educate, shock and delight you.

## A WORD ABOUT CLASSIFICATION

For every animal discussed in this book, there's a scientific name. In many cases, it's the species name, with two parts; for the Lion, for example, the scientific name is *Panthera leo*. Note that both words are in italics. The first word designates the Lion's genus, the second its species. If the species has an English name, that is given first with initial capitals, then the scientific name in brackets, e.g. Lion (*Panthera leo*). If the species has no commonly used English name, its scientific name doesn't go in brackets, e.g. the tiger moth *Bertholdia trigona*.

If the text concerns not just Lions but the three other related big cats too – the Tiger, Leopard and Jaguar – the text will refer to the big cats (note that we're not using the capitals any more; they are only for a single species' English name), genus *Panthera*. A genus (plural genera) may contain one species or hundreds.

The next level in the hierarchy of classification is the family. If we stick with the cats, they belong to the family Felidae. From this level onwards, we drop the italics and use plain text. In the family Felidae there are several genera besides *Panthera*, including *Uncia*, which contains the Snow Leopard (*Uncia nivalis*); *Lynx*, which contains four species of medium-sized, pointy-eared cats; and *Felis*, which contains about eight species of small cats, including the domestic moggie.

Going up from family level we reach order, which in cats is Carnivora. Other families in Carnivora include Canidae (dogs) and Ursidae (bears). Orders are grouped together in a class; in cats the class is Mammalia, and this is the level at which humans (order Primates) and cats are related. Up from class is phylum; for the cats (and us, and all other mammals) it's Chordata, or animals with a spinal cord. Finally, all animal phyla are united in the kingdom Animalia – we've reached the trunk of the tree of animal life. You'll also see the occasional subdivision between these main categories, like 'subphylum' or 'infraclass'.

Why bother with all this malarkey in a book like this, which isn't trying to be a biology textbook? One reason is that scientific names tend to be more consistently used than English names, as scientific names are universal across all languages. If you are intrigued by something you read in this book and want to learn more, you may find you have more luck doing an internet search with the scientific name than the English name. Another reason is that it helps us to understand how closely related animals are to each other and to us.

The final reason is that scientific names are often quite beautiful and their etymology can be very interesting. You may know, for example, that 'Hippopotamus' means 'river horse'. Its scientific name, *Hippopotamus amphibius*, therefore means 'underwater river horse'. A genus of trilobites is called *Aegrotocatellus* – 'sick puppy' (perhaps now it should be changed to something that means 'extinct puppy'). Puffins are *Fratercula*, which means, inexplicably, 'small, female brother', while the birds that have the genus name *Puffinus* are actually shearwaters.

# CHAPTER 1

# EVOLUTIONARY EXCESSES

We live on a planet teeming with a greater diversity of life than most of us would care to imagine, with organisms swarming in the temperate and tropical lands but also surviving in such unpromising environments as the polar ice, deep-sea hydrothermal vents and even Luton. However, the entirety of nature we see today is but a tiny fraction of that which once was. Somewhere between 97 and 99 per cent of all species that have ever lived are now extinct, though some are direct ancestors of modern species. While it's probably a good thing for us that fearsome beasts like the terrible *T. rex*, the immense Haast's Eagle and the famously large-fanged Sabre-toothed Cat are long gone, there are plenty more on the list that are so beautiful, so extraordinary or just so bizarre that it's a shame we only have fossils, stuffed skins or rumour and legend left to remember them by.

## GIVING THE FINGER

The Aye-aye (*Daubentonia madagascariensis*) of Madagascar is a spooky-looking lemur with staring, yellow eyes, huge gremlin ears and a witchy, elongated middle finger, used to probe holes in wood for insect larvae. A similar digital overdevelopment occurred in a tree-dwelling dinosaur, *Therizinosaurus*, which lived somewhere between 170 million and 122 million years ago. As well as its exceptional poking ability, *Therizinosaurus* also had hind feet adapted for gripping and climbing branches, and it is thought by some to be an early precursor to the first birds.

## FOSSIL FANTASIA

You might have heard of the Cambrian Explosion. No dynamite was involved. The Cambrian period of geological time began 542 million years ago, and rocks from this era have preserved a great variety of sea animals, many of which apparently appeared for the first time in a relatively short period. They include early versions of many of the great modern animal groups, like crustaceans, molluscs and even chordates. Also among them are creatures that bear no resemblance whatsoever to anything living today. One of them was the aptly named *Hallucinogenia*, which looked like a worm balanced on a double row of tapered spikes, with a corresponding double row of tentacles protruding from its back. Or maybe it balanced on the tentacles and the spikes were along its back. To be honest, either way up it looks wrong.

## GONE NECKING

One of the great things about evolution is how it produces multiple ways to solve the same problem. Most modern land animals no longer swim with the fishes, but between them they have evolved lots of new methods for continuing to exploit this tasty food source. However, none of them does it quite the way *Tanystropheus* did. This remarkable reptile, which lived about 230 million years ago, had a total length of about 3m, of which more than half was neck. Its small jaws were packed with pointy, interlocking teeth similar to those we see in modern fish-eating reptiles; palaeontologists think it fished by standing at the water's edge, immersing its head and neck and snapping up whatever swam too close. The theory is supported by the fact that *Tanystropheus* possessed an unusually hefty and muscular backside – ballast that provided the bit of it that remained on dry land with extra stability.

## THE BLUE ANTELOPE

There are fewer representatives in the class Mammalia than in the other vertebrate groups, and they're also the least colourful. Not for them the vivid iridescent shades of birds, reptiles, amphibians and fish. One exception was the Blaaubock or Bluebuck (*Hippotragus leucophaeus*), an antelope of southern Africa which, according to the 18th-century explorers who described it, had a distinctly blueish coat, as well as an impressive pair of backswept horns like those of the still-living Sable Antelope, to which it was related. We can't see its famous blue fur for ourselves, though, because the colour faded to dull grey soon after death, and all the Blaaubocks that ever lived are indeed now dead, with just a handful of skins surviving in museums. The species was apparently never very common and disappeared completely in about 1800, not long after the first gun-toting Europeans arrived on the scene. To add insult to extinction, it was not even considered very good to eat.

## BAD TIBBLES

A friend of mine lived in Swaziland for some years and was
able to provide the national mammal recorder with several new
records of mice and other small rodents for the country,
courtesy of the hunting exploits of his cat. Domestic moggies
have made other contributions to scientific research, and it was
a cat which brought the first known specimen of Stephens
Island Wren (*Xenicus lyalli*) to workers on this small island off
the New Zealand coast sometime in 1894. Unfortunately, this
cat and its feline friends had, within months, killed the last
known specimen of the unfortunate bird. The wren, which was
small and flightless, had evolved in an environment where there
are no native predatory mammals and was completely ill-
equipped to cope when humans arrived with their fanged and
furry friends in tow.

## THE FISHAPOD

The fossil record is, inevitably, incomplete as the vast majority of dead organisms were, and still are, eaten by other animals rather than being quietly buried intact in layers of sediment. However, year by year palaeontologists are filling in the gaps and, as this process goes on, they are predicting with increasing accuracy what might be missing and where it might be found. The animal *Tiktaalik* is a great example of this. It was a lobe-finned fish which had the beginnings of wrist-bones and fingers, a precursor to the first four-legged (tetrapod) animals. The fossil record suggested that such an animal would have existed and when and where it would have lived, and in 2004 searchers found it on Ellesmere Island in Canada, in 383-million-year-old rocks.

You wait, one day all the cool fish will be doing this.

## GOING APE

You're not likely to confuse a modern gorilla with any other living animal today. However, things were different 40 million years ago. Meet the chalicotheres (family Chalicotheriidae), a group of powerful-shouldered, long-armed, short-legged, slope-backed, tree-stripping, knuckle-walking... horses. These truly bizarre animals died out 3.5 million years ago, denying the human species the challenging opportunity to attempt to domesticate and ride them.

## 300 MILLION YEARS OF TRILOBITES

It's easy to consider extinct animals as failures, but with a mere 400,000 years under our collective belt, our species is in no position to crow about anything. The famously extinct trilobites (class Trilobita) clocked up a magnificent 300 million years and achieved amazing diversity over that time, but these woodlouse-like marine animals finally threw in the towel towards the end of the Permian period, 250 million years ago, when the formation of the supercontinent Pangaea dramatically reduced the diversity of sea habitats around the world.

## ANTARCTIC ODDITIES

You wouldn't think that Antarctica would be a good place to search for fossils, except those of ancient penguins. But the Earth was much warmer back in the Mesozoic era (250–65 million years ago), and back then the continent was covered in forest (and also was part of the supercontinent Gondwana). Animals that once roamed the now ice-bound continent include an assortment of both herbivorous and carnivorous dinosaurs, other non-dinosaur reptiles, small marsupials and, most startling of all, an ancient kind of sloth.

## ARCHIE'S LEGACY

Most of us have heard of *Archaeopteryx*, the 150-million-year-old bird whose fossils were found in Germany. Prior to this discovery, in the mid-1800s, there was no obvious link between birds and reptiles, but Archie showed intermediate characteristics in abundance. There was the long, bony tail, the sizeable claws on the forelimbs and a mouthful of pointy teeth – all typical of predatory bipedal dinosaurs. However, Archie also possessed long, well-developed flight feathers and was very probably able to glide about with reasonable competence. Subsequent fossil finds have shown that many well-known dinosaurs, including Jurassic Park favourite the *Velociraptor*, possessed simple feathers, which would not have aided flight but more likely helped keep their wearers warm. So it seems that feathers, the defining characteristic of birds, were around long before anything that looked like a bird was.

## CAREER CHANGE

The classic theropod dinosaur (suborder Theropoda) was a fearsome beast, running on two powerful legs and seizing its unfortunate prey between mighty jaws. One group of theropods, however, gave up their predatory ways and went veggie, developing small, Brontosaurus-like heads and jaws, and large scythe-like claws on their forelimbs, which they used to strip foliage from trees. The therasinosaurs lived about 100 million years ago and, like other theropods, wore a coat of fluffy, downy feathers. They probably sat cat-like at the foot of their chosen tree while reaching up to rip off leaves and twigs with those tremendous claws.

## DANGER IN NUMBERS

The world's last Passenger Pigeon (*Ectopistes migratorius*) died in a cage in Cincinnati Zoo in 1914. Just 57 years earlier, a bill put forward to the Ohio State Legislature seeking protection for the species in the wild was turned down, on the grounds that ' no ordinary destruction can lessen them, or be missed from the myriads that are yearly produced'. Whoops.

The pretty and graceful Passenger Pigeon once numbered in the billions and migrated across North America in mile-wide flocks, but deforestation plus massive, rampant hunting (of what must then have seemed to be an inexhaustible supply) put paid to them in just a few decades. They were adapted to exist in huge numbers and at high density, and by the time it was obvious that they had undergone a catastrophic decline, even with protection the remaining flocks were too diminished and fragmented to recover.

## ROAD TO WHALES

Mammals evolved on land but one group made an early return to the seas and is now exquisitely adapted to a watery world. The evolutionary path of the whales is a surprising one; recent fossil discoveries in Pakistan have revealed that the ancestor of modern whales was probably a dog-like but hoof-footed land animal called *Pakicetus*, related to modern deer. The link between *Pakicetus* and the whales is tucked away deep in the middle ear; they share the same bone structure of an obscure bit of skull called the auditory bulla. The same modification shows up in a series of progressively more aquatic and streamlined fossil animals until we reach the modern whales, with their fish-shaped bodies, fins, blowhole, tail flukes and lack of hind legs. But look at a whale skeleton and you'll see tiny rudimentary hind leg bones – a legacy of its land-bound ancestors.

## LAWN MOA

New Zealand separated from the supercontinent Gondwana about 82 million years ago, before there were many mammals on the world scene. It has therefore spent most of its existence as a land of birds (the only native mammals are a couple of bat species). It was, and is, home to an array of birdlife found nowhere else on earth, including many which occupied niches more traditionally utilized by mammals. Across most of the world, the job of grazing the plains and browsing the trees is fulfilled by hoofed mammals – antelopes, deer, cows and so on. In Australia, with only marsupials, kangaroos are the chief native greenery-munchers. In mammal-free New Zealand, a variety of large, chunky and flightless birds called moas evolved and filled the same role. The only thing they had to fear was the equally impressive Haast's Eagle (*Harpagornis moorei*), the largest eagle ever to have lived. The Maori wiped out the moas by the year 1500 and, with its food source gone, the eagle disappeared too (not without eating a few careless Maori first). The moas' relatives, the kiwis, survived by virtue of being small, discreet and nocturnal.

### OLDEST ANIMAL FOSSIL

*Fossils of bacteria date back to 2.8 billion years ago. The earliest true animal fossils, found in 580-million-year-old rocks, are of unclassifiable deep-sea creatures which were sessile (non-moving) and had leaf-like or tube-shaped bodies.*

## THE GIANT ARMOURED NEWT-SNAKE

There are indeed stranger things on earth than most of us can imagine, though it's a shame that some of the strangest are no longer with us. Take *Vancleavea campi*, a 1.2m-long reptile from the Triassic age which looked like a weird hybrid with its long serpentine body, tiny backswept limbs and raised newt-like crest along the upper side of the tail, supported with a row of large, bony, scale-like projections (newts' crests are just soft tissue). This reptile's anatomy suggests it was a swimmer, and its impressive set of fangs indicate that it made life reasonably miserable for other swimming animals.

## REPTILIAN FISHPHINS

The ichthyosaurs (order Ichthyosauria) were among the least
reptilian-looking of all ancient reptiles, at least compared
to the modern reptiles we know and love. 'Ichthyosaur'
translates as 'fish-lizard', but these creatures were also
strikingly dolphinesque in appearance, at least at the front
end, where the jaws formed a projecting beak. In the typical
ichthyosaur all four limbs were flippers, with the front pair
usually much the larger; the tail had fins for propulsion
(vertical like a fish rather than horizontal flukes as in a
dolphin); and the smoothly streamlined body bore a dorsal
fin. Yet they were true air-breathing reptiles. The similarities
between ichthyosaurs (and indeed modern whales and
dolphins) and fish provide a great example of convergent
evolution, whereby unrelated animal lineages develop similar
anatomical features as adaptations to the same habitat.

## MORE THAN ONE WAY TO BE A CAT

Take a look at the skull of a Smilodon or Sabre-toothed Cat
and you'd be hard-pressed to deny that those are an impressive
pair of fangs. But if you know your modern cats,
you might also wonder how on earth it
managed to actually kill
anything with them
– aren't they just too
big for practical
purposes? Analysis
of the jaw bones
suggest that Smilodon,
which lived between 2.5 million
and 10,000 years ago, actually had a
relatively feeble bite compared to
modern (and smaller) cats such as Tigers.
However, it was fantastically stocky,

Well, if you'd taken out
that insurance policy we
recommended...

muscular and (especially) thick-necked. So it's thought that, rather than going for a squeezing bite to the windpipe to suffocate the prey as modern cats do, a Smilodon would wrestle its prey to the ground first and then use its neck power to drive in a fatally deep, down-stabbing bite with the giant fangs. It could therefore potentially take on prey much larger than itself. Whatever the tactic, it seems to have been effective, as large predatory sabre-toothed marsupials, unrelated to the cats, also existed.

## BACK FROM THE DEAD

The coelacanths (two species in the genus *Latimeria*), which can be unkindly but accurately described as big ugly fish, are probably the best-known example we have of 'Lazarus species' – something thought to have gone extinct long ago but then discovered alive and well. It's also an example of stasis in

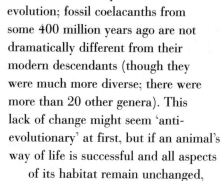

evolution; fossil coelacanths from some 400 million years ago are not dramatically different from their modern descendants (though they were much more diverse; there were more than 20 other genera). This lack of change might seem 'anti-evolutionary' at first, but if an animal's way of life is successful and all aspects of its habitat remain unchanged, stasis is just what we'd expect to see. If it ain't broke—

*And this is your great great great great... hmmmm, do you know how many noughts there are in a million?*

## DINOVENOM

Remember that scene from the first Jurassic Park film, where the cute little *Dilophosaurus* raises its neck frill then spits venom all over a minor character's face? Both the frill and the venom were artistic licence, attributes borrowed from the modern Frill-necked Lizard (*Chlamydosaurus kingii*) and the spitting cobras (genus *Naja*) respectively. Dinosaurs that may truly have possessed venom fangs were those of the genus *Sinornithosaurus*, small and feathery theropods from 125 million years ago. Their long mid-jaw teeth show a distinct groove, ideal for channelling venom and very similar in structure to the fangs of rear-fanged modern snake species like the Boomslang (*Dispholidus typus*).

---

### LARGEST EXTINCT BIRD

*The elephant birds of Madagascar (genus Aepyornis), which lived until the 17th century, were considerably taller and stockier than an Ostrich, with the largest species topping 3m and weighing in at a portly 400kg.*

---

## GOING UNDERGROUND

Travellers on the London Underground should count themselves very lucky, for while they are waiting for the next northbound train to Harrow and Wealdstone, they could be getting bitten by a brand new and exciting species of mosquito. The aptly named *Culex molestans* descends from the overland species *Culex pipiens* but has been isolated from it for decades and has developed distinctly different habits (including, annoyingly, being active all year round rather than just the warmer months), which means the two will no longer interbreed.

## EVOLUTION – DOING IT WRONG?

Evolution works by natural selection preserving the 'best', most resilient members of a varied population. So how did it come up with something as apparently hopeless as the Dodo (*Raphus cucullatus*)? Flightless, dozy, porky, wimpy – surely humanity did the Dodo a favour by ending its pitiful earthly existence in the 1600s? Well, first of all our mental picture of Dodos is based on captive birds, which were overfed to the point of obesity. As for the other charges, Dodos lived only on Mauritius, an island with a limited selection of other species. With no predators, the Dodo (like many other island birds) had no need of flight, and over many generations its pigeon-like ancestors lost the use of their wings, just as some fish which live in deep caves have lost the use of their eyes. This seems like a loss, but growing and maintaining wings and eyes takes energy, so if they are not needed the natural thing is for that energy to be diverted elsewhere.

## GIANTS AND DWARVES

The Dodo is also an example of the phenomenon of 'island gigantism', which occurs mostly in 'prey species' animals that evolve on islands with no predators. Others include a 23kg

...eat the tree, don't eat the tree, eat the tree, don't eat the tree...

rabbit which lived on Minorca, the moas of New Zealand and a bear-sized rodent from Anguilla and Saint Martin in the West Indies. The need to hide from hunters apparently places a constraint on the size such animals will reach, which has been lifted in the island populations. Unfortunately human explorers have shown no respect for the phenomenon and most 'island giants' are now extinct. Islands also play host to unusually small animal forms; 'island dwarfing' happens to species that don't have access to the same rich resources that their relatives on the mainland do. Examples include fossil dwarf elephants from Malta, Sicily and Cyprus, and our own extinct relative *Homo floriensis* (aka the 'hobbit') from Flores in Indonesia.

## SURPRISING SLOTHS

The modern sloth is very decidedly an animal of the treetops, perfectly adapted to a pleasantly lazy arboreal existence. However, the sloth family tree contains a branch of beasts with very different way of life. The genus *Thalassocnus* lived between 25 million and 3 million years ago and was sea-faring sloths, living along the Peruvian coast and feeding on marine vegetation. Like modern sloths they were equipped with impressive claws, not for hanging off branches in their case but to help anchor them to the seabed as they fed.

## THE REAL NESSIE

The real Loch Ness monster could be an Otter, or a bathing Elephant, or a tree, or a small eruption of seismic gas, depending which blurry photograph or speculative explanation you are looking at. However, if by some tiny chance there really is a living, breathing monster in those deep waters, it would probably be a plesiosaur. These reptiles (order Plesiosauria) lived at the same time as the dinosaurs and were well adapted to an aquatic lifestyle, with both fore- and hindlimbs modified into powerful flippers. They had long necks and tails and probably swam with slow grace but quick turns, preying on fish and other suitably sized aquatic animals. The chance of an isolated plesiosaur lineage surviving undetected for 65 million years to give rise to a modern Nessie seems vanishingly small, but maybe, just maybe— (But really, probably not.)

## LARGEST EVER RODENT

*Many animal lineages have super-sized extinct examples. With rodents it's the truly ginormous Phoberomys insolita of South America. Little is known about it, except that it was slightly larger than its better-known relative, the 4.5m, 700kg Phoberomys pattersoni and therefore 15 times larger than the Capybara (Hydrochoerus hydrochaeris), today's largest rodent.*

## BUILD YOUR OWN SEA MONSTER

Palaeontologists tapping out fossils from the Burgess Shale in Canada found a wonderfully rich variety of marine life forms from the Cambrian period, many of them unlike anything alive today. Three examples were a kind of sea sponge-like thing named *Laggania*; the jellyfish *Peytoia*, which resembled a pineapple slice; and *Anomalocaris* (meaning 'strange shrimp'), a segmented, prawn-like animal that the paleontologists never found with its head intact. Further discoveries revealed that these three were not independent creatures at all but were actually all bits of one much larger animal. '*Laggania*' was its body, '*Peytoia*' its mouth and '*Anomalocaris*' one or the other of its weird, downcurved mouth appendages. The animal retained the name *Anomalocaris* and holds the crown for the biggest and probably most ferocious creature in the Cambrian seas.

## HERE BE DRAGONS

If you don't like insects because of the way they fly at you, there's probably a special place in the 'yikes' part of your brain for dragonflies. Big, powerful, fast, direct and rattly in flight and fiercely predatory to boot, they provide a good reason to be grateful you're not a small butterfly. Rewind 300 million years and you could be ducking out of the way of a *Meganeura* – a dragonfly-like insect with a staggering 75cm wingspan. That an insect could reach such a size suggests that the atmosphere of Earth in the Carboniferous period may have been more oxygen-rich than it is today, as the insect method of getting oxygen into its body through spiracles (holes) in its exoskeleton limits maximum body size.

## THROWBACK BODY PARTS

Every so often a human baby is born with a tail. It's a real tail, twitchable and containing bone and muscle. Just as strangely, there are a handful of whales out there with little stumpy projections on their undersides, about where their hind legs

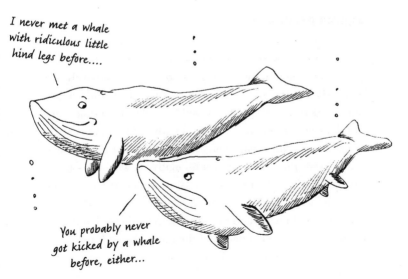

*I never met a whale with ridiculous little hind legs before....*

*You probably never got kicked by a whale before, either...*

would be if whales had hind legs. Traits like these are called atavisms and they probably occur when parts of the genome (an organism's complete set of genetic material) that are normally 'switched off' accidentally become reactivated. In the evolutionary past of humans there are animals with tails, just as whales evolved from land animals with fully developed hind legs, and the genomes of modern humans and modern whales still have tail-making and hind leg-making information respectively; it's just not normally expressed.

## LARGEST EXTINCT LAND MAMMAL

*The mammoths were a diverse group of proboscid (elephant-like) mammals, with the Songhua River Mammoth (Mammuthus sungari) the largest ever. It stood 5.3m tall, was 9.1m long and weighed in the region of 10 tonnes.*

## WALKING PTEROSAURS

They weren't dinosaurs but lived alongside them, or, more precisely, above them. Pterosaurs were spectacular flying reptiles, their membranous wings supported on massively elongated and strengthened fourth 'fingers'. They did not give rise to modern birds, which evolved from theropod dinosaurs and followed a different anatomical path to flight. They came in various sizes, and some were the largest flying animals ever to have lived. Pterosaurs are traditionally shown as coastal fliers, gliding like albatrosses and as incompetent when it comes to moving on land. However, it's now thought that some pterosaurs could walk and even run on four limbs, bearing their weight on the shorter 'fingers' of the forelimbs with the elongated digit and attached membrane swept back behind.

## WHAT A WAG

Related to the idea of atavism is the vestigial trait, which is a body part or behaviour that has lost all or most of its original function. The human appendix is an oft-cited example, while a much lesser-known one is the presence of caudalipuboischiotibialis muscles in the four *Leiopelma* frogs of New Zealand. That long word covers something quite simple; they are the muscles that undertake the vital task of tail-wagging in amphibians that have tails – newts and salamanders. Adult frogs are tailless so most lack the tail-wagging musculature, but it is retained in these four rather primitive species. The Leiopelmas are anatomically almost identical to fossil frogs from 150 million years ago; other odd traits they've retained are round rather than slit-shaped pupils in their eyes and a rather inept and inefficient swimming style.

### LARGEST DINOSAUR

*The longest dinosaur of all could have been a sauropod (think Brontosaurus-shaped beast) called Amphicolias, which is estimated to have reached 60m but is only known from a few bone fragments. Heaviest was probably the 100,000kg Argentinosaurus.*

## MARSUPIAL MASSES

In Australia and New Guinea, where almost all the native non-flying land mammals are marsupials, an impressive degree of convergent evolution can be seen, with pouch-bearing equivalents of a whole range of the more familiar placental mammals from the other continents. The Sugar Glider (*Petaurus breviceps*) looks just like a flying squirrel. The Thylacine (*Thylacinus cynocephalus*), now sadly extinct, is a dead (literally) ringer for a fox or mini-wolf. Marsupial moles (genus *Notoryctes*) are as velvety-furred, short-sighted and adept at digging as their namesakes, in particular the golden moles (family Chrysochloridae) of Africa.

---

## FASTEST DINOSAUR

*Until we send a scientist with a stopwatch back in time, we can't be sure. Studies of stride length of fossilized footprints suggest that the ostrich-like ornithomimids (literally 'bird-imitators') could race along at 40km an hour. However, more recent sophisticated computer simulations put the theropod Compsognathus on top of the podium at 64km an hour.*

---

## MARSUPIALS LOST

Not every marsupial lives in New Guinea or Australia. A few are found elsewhere on Earth, such as various possums (family Didelphidae) in North and South America, and the Sulawesi Bear Cuscus (*Ailurops ursinus*) of Indonesia. How did they get there? It's believed that in the early days of mammal evolution both marsupials and the pouchless placental mammals appeared at about the same time, and both spread across the world via land bridges and other now-lost continental connections. However, the placentals proved much better at the game of life than their pouched cousins on all continents except Australia (where it's thought that the lower marsupial metabolism aided survival in the prevailing hot climate). Elsewhere, only a few marsupial species still exist, honed by competition with the placentals into formidable survivors. The Virginia Opossum (*Didelphis virginiana*) is one of North America's most widespread and successful mammals, rubbing shoulders with rats, Raccoons and other inner-city wildflie.

## HORNY BEAST

The most impressive set of antlers ever to grace a stag's head belonged to the Irish Elk or Giant Deer (*Megaloceros giganteus*) and measured more than 3.5m from tip to tip. The deer itself was (along with Alaskan Moose) the largest deer ever to live, but even though it stood 2m tall at the shoulder, its antlers still looked disproportionately huge compared with those of smaller deer species. It was theorized that 'runaway sexual selection' was responsible for both the antler size and the species' extinction 7,000 years ago: the females selected the most large-antlered males to father their offspring, and eventually the antlers became so large, heavy and unwieldy that their wearers couldn't cope with them. However, palaeontologist Stephen Jay Gould carried out a comparative study that showed that large-bodied deer can manage perfectly well with proportionately larger antlers. It's now thought that, yet again, hunting by humans caused the extinction of this most impressive animal.

## DARWIN'S MOCKINGBIRDS

Much is made of the Galapagos finches (they are actually not true finches but related to the tanagers) and their role in the formulation of Darwin's theory of evolution. However, it was actually the island's mockingbirds that caught his attention first. Four very closely related species live on the Galapagos, and although the islands lie in close proximity the different species stick to their own islands. Noticing this, Darwin wondered whether they all had a single common ancestor, a notion that was to become a cornerstone of the theory of evolution.

---

### OLDEST FOSSIL BIRD

*Since the transition from dinosaur to modern bird involved several key anatomical changes, it's hard to be specific here. However, the oldest fossil dinosaur that has feather impressions is Sinosauropteryx prima, found in China in rocks about 123 million years old.*

---

## TOADILY UNIQUE

Take a look at a picture of a Mexican Burrowing Toad (*Rhinophrynus dorsalis*) when you get the chance. It's not that exciting to look at and there's nothing that weird in its lifestyle either – it eats insects, shelters in burrows and likes rain. There are definitely stranger-looking anurans (that's the fancy term for frogs and toads) out there and we'll be meeting some of them later. But the Mexican Burrowing Toad is special, in that its lineage has evolved independently of other anurans for a very, very long time – 190 million years. It has therefore achieved a mind-boggling level of genetic distinctiveness. This means that you and I have more in common, genetically speaking, with a manatee, vampire bat, Golden-rumped Elephant Shrew or hedgehog than a Mexican Burrowing Toad does with any other frog or toad.

---

## DENSEST DINOSAUR

*Dinosaurs are often characterized as slow-witted, a charge probably unfairly levelled at the likes of Velociraptor. However, Stegosaurus, with its 80g brain controlling a body the size of a bus, was probably not the sharpest tool in the drawer.*

---

# CHAPTER 2

# BIZARRE BODIES

$tar Trek$ is a fantastic invention but one area where it falls
down is the lack of variety in its alien species. With a whole
galaxy of inhabited worlds to choose from, you might expect
intelligent life to have taken a few forms other than the
standard humanoid body shape, but apparently not. More than
400 different species appear in the *Star Trek* films and shows,
and nearly all of them look like *Homo sapiens*, only with
variably knobbly foreheads. *Star Trek* does have an excuse in
that many of the aliens have to interact with ordinary humans
– talking to them, walking with them and, often, kissing them.
Sticking a prosthetic forehead on an actor is much cheaper than
creating a brand new CGI life form. However, even if this were
not the case and the show had the means and inclination to
produce the strangest and most 'alienesque' beings conceivable,
the show's makers face another problem – dreaming up
something to rival the animal oddities that already live right
here on planet Earth. Who'd be a sci-fi writer?

## RUSH OF BLOOD TO THE HEAD

The Giraffe (*Giraffa camelopardalis*) has a heart that weighs
20 times as much as its brain. That huge muscular blood-
pumper is the way it is so it can get blood all the way up the
prodigiously long neck, but the pressure thus generated is twice
that of a less comedically proportioned mammal of the same
weight, so the Giraffe needs a way to reduce its blood pressure
so its brain doesn't explode when the head is lowered down.
The solution is a *rete mirabile* ('wonderful net') of densely

packed, variably sized and circuitous blood vessels in its neck, which kicks in to slow the blood flow down whenever the animal splays its legs and lowers its head to drink.

## JUNK IN THE TRUNK

With a name like Fat-tailed False Antechinus, this cute little marsupial from Australia hardly needs any other attribute to earn itself a place in a book about animal oddities. Its scientific name (*Pseudantechinus macdonnellensis*) is just as much of a mouthful, but there's something even stranger about the Fat-tailed False Antechinus – it uses its tail as a food store. The tail is carrot-shaped (widest where it meets the body) and in a well-nourished Fat-tai… FTFA is thick and heavy with stored fat, to be called upon when times get tough. It's therefore functionally rather like a camel's hump (in the Dromedary) or humps (in the Bactrian Camel). The Monito del Monte (*Dromicerops gliroides*), a South American marsupial, not only stores fat in its tail but can also use the prehensile tail tip to help it climb.

## LARGEST AMPHIBIAN

*While it's appealing to imagine a frog the size of a warthog, the largest amphibian is inevitably one of the ones with a tail. The Chinese Giant Salamander (Andrias davidianus) can reach 1.8m in length. Just for fun, the biggest frog is the Goliath Frog (Conraua goliath), which can weigh 3kg. That's about the same as the world's smallest antelope, the Royal Antelope, which, like the Goliath Frog, lives in West Africa.*

Well, hello there...

## SKIN AND BONES

Ever heard the expression 'greenstick fracture'? It means a bone break that's messy and splintered, as you would observe if you broke a fleshy, living 'green' twig, as opposed to the neat, clean snap of a dry, brown dead one, not that the bone in question is actually green. However, there *are* animals with green bones, and if you don't believe that you can easily check for yourself without hurting the animal in question, because it's half transparent. Glass frogs of the genus *Cochranella*, which live in Central and South America, are tiny critters with transparent skin on their undersides, through which you can see their internal bits and pieces and also their strange green bones. The combination of clear skin and green bones could help camouflage the frogs in their treetop habitats.

## THE FOUR-LEGGED INSECT

Next time someone mentions that insects have six legs give them a long hard stare and ask if they've ever taken a close look at a Red Admiral (*Vanessa atalanta*), Monarch (*Danaus plexippus*) or Painted Lady (*Vanessa cardui*) butterfly. These species, like the rest of the 6,000-strong butterfly family Nymphalidae, are quadrupeds, supporting their weight on just four legs. The first pair of legs is reduced to a couple of tiny, bristly stumps tucked up against the butterfly's head. They may have a sensory function, helping females to find the right plants on which to lay their eggs: butterflies have the interesting ability of being able to taste things through their body hair.

### SMALLEST AMPHIBIANS AND REPTILES

*Several tropical frogs, including representatives of the genera Eleutherodactylus and Psyllophryne, barely reach 10mm. Two tiny geckos from the genus Sphaerodactylus share the accolade of smallest reptile, measuring 16mm from snout to tail tip.*

## THE TAIL THAT ISN'T

It's perhaps the most ostentatious display in the animal kingdom. The Peacock (*Pavo cristatus*) stands resplendent, framed by the numerous bright blue 'eyes' revealed on the spread green feathers of his semi-circular nuptial fan, and shivers the whole lot in an alluring shimmy – what peahen could say no to that? The funny thing is that this glorious train of feathers is not the Peacock's tail. If you walk round to the back of the displaying bird you can see his actual tail feathers: shortish, plain brown and sturdy-looking, fanned out behind the colourful ones and propping up the whole structure. The fancy ones are the uppertail coverts, which in most other birds are small and short, forming a little pad of feathers right at the base of the tail proper.

### CARRYING A TORCH

Having some sort of portable light-casting device is often useful, and in the film *ET* the eponymous alien went one better, with a light-emitting fingertip. On land, there are a few real animals that can light themselves up, such as fireflies (family Lampyridae). In deep seas, where little sunlight penetrates, bioluminescence is common among many different animal groups. One unusual example comes from the stoplight loosejaw fish (genus *Malacosteus*), which produce (and can see) red light, unlike most other deep-sea fishes, which can only see the blue light that predominates at these depths. This enables them to see without being seen – a great advantage.

### A NOSE FOR TALENT

Elephant skulls look especially weird to us because the most distinctive parts of the living animal – the long trunk and big, flappy ears – are absent. The trunk of an elephant is analogous to our nose plus upper lip and contains some 40,000 different muscles, making it capable of very free movement and impressively fine and delicate control, as well as delivering a tremendously powerful whack. It is used to rip up foliage and pass it into the mouth and to suck up water, which can either be squirted into the mouth or sprayed across the back to help cool the animal down. The trunk is also used in displays of dominance and to deliver caresses in more tender situations between friends or mother and baby.

## HALF-ASLEEP

What would happen to a human who fell asleep underwater? At best, a rapid, very unpleasant and spluttery awakening, at worst, drowning. Dolphins and whales (order Cetacea) can hold their breath underwater much longer than we can but still need to come to the surface to breathe, making sleep a risky business. They counter this by sleeping with one half of their brains at a time. In this state, which takes up about a third of each 24-hour period, they are alert enough to come to the surface when it's time for the next breath but are otherwise more or less inactive.

---

### SMALLEST MAMMAL

There are two contenders for this title – the Etruscan Shrew (*Suncus etruscus*) from southern Europe and the Bumblebee Bat (*Craseonycteris thonglongyai*) of South-east Asia. The shrew is the lightest, with the smallest adults a mere 1.3g, while the bat weighs 2g but has a shorter body.

---

## HARD-ASS

Wombats (family Vombatidae) are the marsupial world's answer to badgers, or maybe bears, or maybe neither. They are short-legged, tailless and very stocky, and spend much of their time digging an extensive network of burrows (female wombats have backward-facing pouches so they don't choke their babies with flying soil when digging). If chased down a burrow by a Dingo (*Canis lupus dingo*) or a Tasmanian Devil (*Sarcophilus harrisii*), the wombat's retreating rear presents a large target, but that big behind is packed with tough cartilage, making it very difficult for the predator to grab. If the predator persists, the wombat can also deliver a strong kick with its back legs.

## SHEEP IN WOLF'S CLOTHING...

They say imitation is the sincerest form of flattery. Maybe that's true in humans, but in animals mimicry is often a cunning disguise, to make an animal look more dangerous than it is. Batesian mimicry is the phenomenon whereby animal A, which is harmless, looks like animal B, which isn't, and therefore animal A benefits from predators' learned avoidance of animal B. A familiar example comes from the hoverflies, which have a wasp-like, black and yellow stripy pattern. In the UK, the Buff Ermine moth (*Spilosoma luteum*), a delicious snack for any bird, looks a lot like the White Ermine moth (*Spilosoma lubricipeda*), which tastes horrible. Because the Buff Ermine emerges from its pupa slightly later than the White Ermine, many birds that encounter a Buff Ermine will already have had a bad experience with a White Ermine and will give it a wide berth.

## ... AND WOLF IN WOLF'S CLOTHING

When two equally nasty species resemble each other, that's called Müllerian mimicry. Unlike with Batesian mimicry, where only the mimic benefits, in Müllerian mimicry both are mimics of each other and both benefit. One impressive case of Müllerian mimicry is provided by the Viceroy butterfly (*Limenitis archippus*) of North America, which looks almost exactly the same as the Monarch butterfly (*Danaus plexippus*), although the two are not closely related. Both are distasteful to predators, so a bird that has spat out a Monarch on Tuesday is not likely to attack a Viceroy on Wednesday, and vice versa. Viceroy populations living in other areas that have no Monarchs have adapted to look like the Queen butterfly (*Danaus*

*gilippus*) or the Soldier butterfly (*Danaus eresimus*), depending
which occurs in their area.

### SMALLEST AND LARGEST INSECTS

*With a name much longer than itself, the parasitic wasp
Dicopomorpha echmepterygis is the smallest known insect, males
measuring just 0.139mm. You could fit quite a few of them
along the back of a Phobaeticus chani stick insect, which may
grow to 56.7cm long. The heaviest insect on record is a larval
Goliath Beetle (Goliathus goliatus), which can reach 115g (adults
are considerably lighter).*

## FUZZY FROG...

Frogs, though certainly often cute, aren't really what you'd think
of as cuddly. One species that is (well, sort of) is the Hairy Frog
(*Trichobatrachus robustus*) of central Africa. It isn't hairy all
over, just on its sides and thighs, and it's only breeding males
who grow this 'hair'; females and non-breeding males are
ordinary-looking, smooth-skinned frogs. The hair is actually fine
extensions of the amphibian's skin – dermal papillae. As frogs
can absorb some oxygen from water through their skin,
dramatically increasing its surface area in this way means the
frog can stay comfortably underwater much longer. This is a
boon for the male Hairy Frog, as after mating it's his job to take
care of the frogspawn. Hairy Frogs have another unique feature
– bony 'claws' which break through the skin of the 'fingertips'
when the frog is seized by a predator (or a naturalist).

## ... AND FURRY CRAB

We've learned that what looks like fur on a frog is actually lots
of delicate outgrowths of skin. Hair or bristles on invertebrates

are called setae, and few possess more luxuriant setae than those which grow on the long forelimbs of the wonderfully peculiar Yeti Crab (*Kiwa hirsuta*). Only discovered in 2005, this crab hangs around hydrothermal vents deep in the south Pacific. Its flowing golden locks contain filamentous bacteria (rod-shaped bacteria which don't divide properly and form long continuous strands), which are thought to remove toxins from the volatile, chemical-rich waters where the crab makes its home.

---

### LARGEST REPTILE

*Now dinosaurs are a thing of the past, the largest reptile is the Saltwater Crocodile of Australia (Crocodylus porosus), the biggest on record being 6.3m long and weighing 1,360kg. The largest Green Anaconda (Eunectes murinus) was a shade longer than this at 7m but weighed just 250kg.*

---

### NEARLY LEGLESS

In Greek mythology, a siren was a winged woman, who sang sailors to their doom. It's hard to make the leap from that to a fat, peculiar salamander in North America but such are the vagaries of animal names. Sirens (family Sirenidae) are unlike other salamanders in several respects, most noticeably because they have no hind legs and fully formed but dismally tiny front legs. They move by a combination of snake-like wiggling and heaving themselves along with their front legs. One nifty trick they possess is that of surviving droughts by sheltering inside a sort of casing made from their own dead skin and dried-up skin slime. This ability contributes towards an impressive 25-year lifespan. Also, there is one species that grows to an eye-catching 95cm.

## GOT IT LICKED

Woodpeckers have a number of physical adaptations which enable them to pursue their high-impact lifestyle. One of the less obvious ones is the unusual anatomy of the woodpecker tongue. Bird tongues are bony up to the tip and in woodpeckers are further modified with barbs and a sharp point to help them skewer fat insect larvae and haul them out of holes drilled in tree trunks and branches. Perhaps oddest of all is that in the longest-tongued species the tongue-extending muscles extend in a loop around the back of the bird's skull and anchor just behind the upper base of the bill. When not in use the muscles have lots of 'give' but when contracted they fire the tongue out to a prodigious length, in some species several times longer than the bird's bill.

## THE PHOTOSYNTHETIC SLUG

It's easy enough to tell plants from animals, right? Even down
to the cellular level it can be done by looking for chloroplasts
(the tiny objects inside plant cells which contain the chlorophyll
for photosynthesis). But even this rule has its exception, in the
wibbly wobbly form of *Elysia chlorotica*, a sea slug of the
Atlantic. The slug is green and eats algae. It doesn't just break
the algae down for sustenance though but 'steals' not only its
chloroplasts but also part of its genetic code. The chloroplasts
reside in the cells lining the slug's gut, where they do what
chloroplasts everywhere do – convert sunlight into useable
energy. The algal genes appropriated by the slug enable it to
make the proteins necessary to keep the chloroplasts in good
working order.

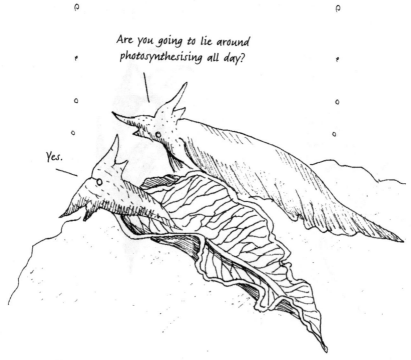

## TELESCOPE EYES AND A SEE-THROUGH HEAD

You know how it is. You need to be able to see the bio-luminescent jellyfish in order to eat it but those tentacles can really sting your eyes. This is apparently the problem that is solved by the bizarre head anatomy of the deep-sea fish *Macropinna microstoma*. It has tubular, highly moveable eyes, which are equipped with massive lenses to make the of the feeble light levels available in the deep waters it inhabits. Those big, weird eyes are protected behind the fish's prominent bulbous forehead, which is fluid-filled and transparent, like a skull-shaped shield, keeping the eyes safe from wayward tentacles.

---

### LONGEST TENTACLES

*The Lion's Mane Jellyfish (Cyanea capillata) is a huge example of jellyfish-kind, and what must have been one of the biggest ever was found washed up in Massachusetts Bay in 1870 – its tentacles stretched 36.5m (longer than a Blue Whale).*

---

### THE ORIGINAL ALIEN

Remember when we first get a proper look at the titular beast in horror sci-fi film *Alien*? One of the most startling things about this fearsome, slime-coated creature is its forward-firing 'inner' mouth, which shoots out like a tongue to chew a hole in its prey after its proper mouth is opened. The inspiration for this came from a much smaller animal, the dragonfly nymph. Dragonflies spend their formative months or years as wingless water creatures, rushing after prey like tadpoles and even tiny fish, manoeuvring around on six strong legs and propelling themselves by expelling jets of water. They catch prey by firing forward their lower lip (labium); it shoots out at great speed,

47

reaches well beyond the head and has gripping appendages at the tip to seize the unfortunate victim.

### DISCO SQUID

What's better than a cute 7cm squid? A cute 7cm squid that's covered in little flashing blue lights, of course. The Firefly Squid (*Watasenia scintillans*), like many other animals that can produce bioluminescence, has organs called photophores on its body, in which a chemical reaction occurs to generate light (though in some other bioluminescent animals, the light is produced by bacteria).The Firefly Squid puts on an impressive light show; with photophores all over its body right to the tips of its tentacles, it can show up as a squid-shaped outline of light but can also switch its lights on and off in a rippling pattern – impressive to the opposite sex and a good way to break up its outline and confuse predators.

---

### SMALLEST VERTEBRATE

This is a 7.9mm fish rejoicing in a name much longer than itself, Paedocypris progenetica of Indonesia.

---

### REGENERATION

The long, swishing tail of a lizard is a tempting target for a predator, but an attacker who grabs just this bit may find that it's all they get. Many lizards and some salamanders can drop their tails when necessary, a process called autotomy. When the tail is grabbed, the lizard contracts muscles that break a vertebra along the tail, so it snaps off. A sphincter muscle on the tail stump then tightens to minimize blood loss, while the severed tail section continues to wriggle enticingly for some time, hopefully distracting the predator for long enough for the lizard to escape. The lost bones are gone forever but a new tail tip made of cartilage will eventually regrow.

## SHARING ADAM'S APPLE

We humans have a physiological trait that was once thought to be unique – a descended larynx. Other mammals have the larynx or voice box high in the throat, where it protects the windpipe from accidental inhalation of food while the animal is feeding. In humans, it moves down to a lower position as we grow up, forming the 'Adam's apple' bulge in the throat. The lower it goes the more deep sounds we can make. So we have better vocal abilities than most other animals and (unfortunately) we are also better at choking to death. The descended larynx, however, is not unique to humans, as anyone who ever took a look at a male Fallow Deer (*Dama dama*) would agree. The deer's pronounced Adam's apple enables him to make loud, deep barks and rumbles, which help him intimidate other males during the rutting season. Research has also now shown that many other deep-voiced animals have larynxes that bob downwards while they're making their growls, roars or grunts.

---

### LARGEST BUTTERFLY

*The Queen Alexandra's Birdwing (Ornithoptera alexandrae), a fine-looking creature from Papua New Guinea, has a wingspan of up to 31cm and weighs a whopping 12g.*

---

## BRAIN-EATERS

Tunicates (subphylum Urochordata), also known as sea squirts or sea cucumbers, look (and behave) more like plants than animals. Actually they are quite closely related to us, belonging (according to most biologists) to the phylum Chordata. They start life as free-swimming, tadpole-like larvae but then fix on to a rock and change shape and lifestyle, secreting a covering or 'tunic' of cellulose (no other animal can produce this tough material – it's more typical of plants) to protect them from predators in their new motionless forms. They will stay put for the rest of their lives, filtering out particles of food from the sea water around them. Each tunicate's cerebral ganglion, a cluster of nerve cells which controlled their movement as larvae, is now no longer needed and so gets digested, meaning these animals eat their own brains.

## LONGEST FEATHER

*This grows out of the bum of a male Reeve's Pheasant (Syrmanticus reevesii) – the tail feathers can be 2.4m long.*

## PORTABLE HAIR CARE

Efficiently scratching your face with your toenails is a feat that's beyond even the most supple human. Most other mammals do deal with face and neck itches this way, though they need to be careful when they do it. The Felou Gundi (*Felovia vae*), a guinea pig-like rodent from West Africa, has a more significant problem than most. It possesses very thick, very large and very strong claws to help it keep a grip on the smooth rocks of its desert habitat. It also has extremely soft, fine but dense fur, which helps protect it both from chilling and from overheating in the harsh desert climate. Those big claws would quickly wreck that delicate coat, so the Felou Gundi has a couple of built-in hairbrushes on its hind paws – comb-like bristles on the toes, which are perfect for the gentle grooming its fine fur requires.

## WALKING FISH

The evolutionary story tells us that certain fish acquired, over generations, the ability to walk on land, thus eventually giving rise to land vertebrates. This sounds fanciful to some, until you point out that a variety of walking fish can be seen alive and well today, though not all are closely linked with the same lineages that gave rise to the first amphibians. The best-known modern walking fish are probably the mudskippers (subfamily Oxudercinae), which can be found from Africa across to Australia. They can hop about happily on land for extended periods, supporting their weight on their pectoral fins and 'breathing' oxygen through their wet skins. They can even scramble up to modest heights in the mangrove trees that emerge from their watery habitats.

## STICK AROUND

Wet adhesion doesn't sound very pleasant, but numerous species of insects and tree frogs would be lost without it. It's the means by which two smooth surfaces stick together if there's a bit of liquid between them and it enables these small animals to walk on or cling to vertical surfaces and even go upside-down. The same technique is used by a couple of bats from Madagascar – the sucker-footed bats (genus *Myzopoda*). These petite bats roost (the right way up, unusually for bats) on large, upright fan-palm leaves, hanging on with the flattened pads at their wrists and also on their little hind legs. The liquid that they secrete to hold them there is described by scientists, enigmatically, as 'modified sweat'.

## FOREVER YOUNG

It's not in the same league as hamsters and gerbils but the Axolotl (*Ambystoma mexicanum*) is a fairly popular pet among those who like exotic animals and don't mind taking the necessary care to keep its tank water at the right temperature and chemical balance. It looks like a somewhat squashed and sluggish newt, with a frill of feathery gills around its head. Those gills are the key to what's particularly strange about this already quite strange-looking salamander – it displays the property of neoteny, which means it can become fully sexually mature without ever completing its metamorphosis to a full adult salamander with the ability to breathe air. Captive-bred Axolotls will never undergo metamorphosis without extensive environmental alteration, and the process is extremely dangerous for them as well as drastically life-shortening if it succeeds.

## WHEEL OF FORTUNE

The Ancient Greeks came up with the striking symbol of Ouroboros – a snake or dragon eating its own tail and forming a wheel or ring shape with its body – to express endless renewal. The real-world Ouroboros is the Armadillo Lizard (*Cordylus cataphractus*) of southern Africa. It looks like a normal enough lizard most of the time, but give it a fright and it takes its tail tip in its mouth to form a wheel shape. This posture protects its vulnerable underside and also causes the numerous rows of spikes along its back and tail to stand out, transforming it into a spiny ball that will surely stick painfully in the throat of any would-be predator.

## WHAT GOES NINETY-NINE... BONK?

It's a centipede with a wooden leg, of course, but this timeless joke doesn't work with real-life centipedes, unfortunately. They may have as few as 30 legs or as many as 342 but no centipede can ever have 100 legs, because the leg pairs always come in an odd number. Millipedes don't have as many legs as their name suggests either, though the average millipede has more legs than the average centipede, with two pairs on each body segment (centipedes have just one pair per segment). The millipede that comes closest to the 1,000 mark is *Illacme plenipes* from California, adult females of which may possess up to 750 legs.

## CROWNING GLORY

As of 2009, the mammal with the longest hair in the world was Xie Qiuping, a Chinese lady whose tresses were measured at 5.627m in 2004. If we exclude humans, who after all can cheat by tying up their hair to protect it from natural wear and tear, the longest-haired mammals tend to be those that live in the coldest places, for obvious reasons. Snow Leopards (*Uncia uncia*) have longer fur than the lowland big cats. Polar Bears (*Ursus maritimus*) are so well insulated by their dense pelts and subcutaneous fat that they hardly show up to infrared cameras. The longest-haired of all is the Musk Ox (*Ovibos moschatus*), whose 0.6m guard hairs help keep out the Arctic chill.

...some long layers, a choppy fringe... oh, and about an inch off my beard, please.

## THE BIRD THAT THINKS IT'S A MAMMAL

Kiwis (genus *Apteryx*) come from New Zealand, a land without any native mammals, save a few species of bats. Therefore many ecological niches associated elsewhere with mammals were occupied in New Zealand by birds, and the birds became somewhat mammal-like in the process of convergent evolution. Kiwis are probably analogous to hedgehogs or other insectivorous, nocturnal, snuffling creatures of the undergrowth. They are rotund, heavy with short, sturdy legs, have simple, hair-like feathers and have poor eyesight but a very keen sense of smell (enhanced by having nostrils at the bill tip rather than close to the base as in other birds). Kiwis are also the only birds with two functional ovaries, mammal-style; in other birds only the left ovary ever fully develops.

### LARGEST FISH

It's a shark but luckily for us not one of the toothy kind that eats surfers. The largest Whale Shark (Rhincodon typus) on record was 12.65m long and weighed possibly as much as 21 tonnes. A lot of plankton must have gone into the making of such an impressive beast. The largest bony fish (which excludes sharks as they are supported by cartilage rather than bone) is the oarfish Regalecus glesne, sometimes called the 'King of Herrings', which can reach 11m or more.

## GETTING INKED

Squids have bizarre bodies, at least they seem that way to us with our measly one heart (squids have three) and four limbs (squids have eight arms and two tentacles). One of the most unusual attributes of these marine molluscs is their ability to squirt out a cloud of black ink when they are under attack, creating an aquatic equivalent of a smokescreen the same size as their own body, behind which they make their escape while the would-be predator struggles to work out what's going on. The ink comes from a gland at the animal's rear end and is made almost entirely of melanin – the same stuff that gives our skin its colour. The ink of cuttlefish, which are related to squids, is the kind used to make 'squid-ink pasta', a glossy black dish which tastes as... interesting as it looks.

---

### BIGGEST BRAIN

*As a proportion of total body weight, humans are the brainiest. The absolute biggest brain does not belong to the Blue Whale this time but to its smarter little cousin, the Sperm Whale (Physeter macrocephalus), with 9kg of thinking material. Sperm Whales are hunters; it obviously takes more brain power to catch squids than it does to hoover up 3,500kg of tiny krill every day.*

---

### SAW POINT

Wouldn't it be great if, instead of a nose, you had a huge, multi-toothed saw attached to your face? The snout or rostrum of a sawfish (family Pristidae) is greatly elongated, flattened and toothed along its sides with denticles, which are modified hard and pointy scales (denticles are also found on the bodies of sharks and other related fish). The sawfish's mouth is small and on the underside of its head, so it's not immediately obvious how the saw, ferocious though it is, helps the fish catch its prey. The answer is not very sophisticated: when the sawfish spots a small fish or other suitable victim, it rushes at it, slashing its saw wildly from side to side. A few blows will probably cripple or even dismember the prey, and the sawfish can eat what's left at its leisure. The saw isn't just an offensive weapon though; it also has electroceptors and motion-sensitive pores, to help it locate crustaceans and other prey on the ocean floor.

## DON'T EAT ME

Animals don't, as a rule, stand around and let other animals kill and eat them. The Black Jumping Salamander (*Pseudoeurycea nigra*) of North America has a particularly wide variety of ways to avoid being eaten. For a start, it is slim, long-legged and very agile for a salamander, able to climb speedily using all four 'hands' and also its prehensile tail. It is also capable of impressive leaps. It may choose to lie immobile and hope it doesn't get seen by the predator, or if it clearly has been spotted it will perform a startling coiling-and-flipping display. If all else fails and the salamander is grabbed, its bad-tasting skin secretions and poison-producing parotoid glands may mean it quickly gets dropped, while it also possesses the ability to detach its tail.

---

### LONGEST ANIMAL

The Bootlace Worm (*Lineus longissimus*) of the North Sea can reach more than 55m; Blue Whales (*Balaenoptera musculus*), the largest animals overall, only stretch to about 33m.

---

## GIRLS WILL BE BOYS

If Sigmund Freud had been a hyena, his ideas about penis envy would have made a lot more sense. Female Spotted Hyenas (*Crocuta crocuta*) are endowed with enlarged clitorises that are the same size and shape as the penises of their male counterparts, and the rest of their lady-parts are structured to look just like the male scrotum. Their unusual anatomy means they have a particularly hard time when giving birth but also allows them to have absolute control over who they mate with, as copulation is impossible without full female cooperation.

## TWO FEET GOOD

One of the things that we like to think separates us humans from the rest of the mammals is our bipedalism. Except it doesn't – plenty of other mammals get about on two legs. The obvious ones are the kangaroos and wallabies, which bound along on their big muscular hind legs. Looking like miniature kangaroos, the jerboas (gerbil-like rodents from Asia and north Africa) locomote in a similar manner, as does the peculiar Springhare (*Pedetes capensis*) from southern Africa. The Giant Pangolin (*Manis gigantea*), a strange ant-eating animal which looks a bit like a huge pine cone, walks competently on two or four legs. The other great apes (besides ourselves) can all walk on two legs though usually choose not to, while the 13 species of lemurs in the family Indridae spend most of their time in trees but traverse the ground with impressive two-legged bounds, holding their arms out high before them.

Ow!

## IS IT A STARFISH? IS IT A CRAB?

No, it's a Mimic Octopus (*Thaumoctopus mimicus*), the most deceptive creature in the sea. Having a highly flexible body and the ability to change its skin colour enables this Indonesian creature to effectively imitate 15 or more different sea animals, including sea anemones, cnidarians (aka jellyfish), sea snakes and a variety of fish. Its many different faces are utilized primarily to deter predators, and its choice of form is influenced by the kind of predator around at the time. It also uses its mimicry to attract prey for itself; assuming the shape of a crab, for example, may attract another octopus, which the Mimic Octopus will then attack.

### ANIMAL WITH THE LONGEST TONGUE

*The Blue Whale wins this one – and most other 'biggest' records – by virtue of being the largest of all animals, with a 4m (and 2.7-tonne) tongue. Relative to body size, the longest mammal tongue belongs to the Tube-lipped Nectar Bat, which uses its 8.5cm tongue (1.5 times longer than its body) to pollinate a particular Ecuadorean flower. Some chameleon species have proportionately even longer tongues.*

## FLIP SIDE

If you were a fan of the TV programme *Robot Wars*, you'll remember that the best robots all had a 'Srimech', or self-righting mechanism, for when they are flipped on their backs by a rival robot. Some animals are in dire need of a similar gadget: beetles and tortoises, for example, can really struggle to right themselves if turned over (don't do it, it's unkind) thanks to their high, rounded and rigid backs. The horseshoe crabs (family Limulidae), which don't look much like crabs and are actually related to spiders, have a similar shape problem with their round carapaces. However, they possess an elegant self-righting mechanism. Their long, fine, pointed tails (telson), normally used to steer them as they swim, can be braced hard against the ground to flip them over if necessary.

---

## LARGEST CRUSTACEAN

*Most crustaceans are pretty small by our standards. Not so the Japanese Spider Crab (Macrocheira kaempferi) with its 60cm body and 4m leg-span.*

---

## TENREC OF MANY FACES

Take a selection of unusual small mammals from Africa and Madagascar. One looks like a shrew, with long, pointy nose and tiny eyes and ears. Another is a perfect match for a hedgehog, covered in spines with a blunt little face. A third is a perfect miniature otter, complete with powerful, long tail, blunt and much-bewhiskered muzzle and a dense, silky, waterproof coat. Number four looks like a fuzzy mouse, with big eyes and ears, dainty nose and soft grey fur. The fifth has a long, flexible snout like an elephant-shrew but also a striking ruff of orange spines, making it look like nothing else on earth. The tenrecs (family Tenrecidae) are remarkable in their diversity, with convergent evolution shaping them to look like a whole range of other mammal groups.

## CHEMISTRY SET

One of the most impressive defences against predation is that employed by the bombardier beetles, which make up part of the family Carabidae. When threatened, a bombardier beetle ejects a jet of bad-smelling and boiling hot liquid from its rear end, making a loud popping sound. The combination of startling sound, heat and stink are enough to deter almost any attacker. The explosion is created when two chemicals – hydroquinone and hydrogen peroxide – are secreted in the beetle's abdomen. They mix with each other in the presence of catalysing enzymes and some water in a sort of combustion chamber, producing a strong oxidizing reaction. An outlet valve releases the boiling fluid, while the inward valve closes off so the beetle doesn't blow itself up.

---

### SMALLEST BIRD

*This is the 5cm Bee Hummingbird (Mellisuga helenae), which weighs 1.8g and would not look oversized as an adornment on the non-writing end of a pencil. If we subscribe to the view that birds are dinosaurs, then it is also the smallest dinosaur ever to have lived.*

---

## TOOTH OF THE UNICORN

The Narwhal (*Monodon monoceros*) doesn't look much like a horse, being a rather podgy small whale. However, it does have a long, spiralling horn thing poking out from its face, hence its nickname of 'sea unicorn'. The 'horn-thing' is in fact a tooth (or tusk – the usual name for a poky-out tooth in an animal) and is the Narwhal's only visible tooth in fact. Both male and female Narwhals grow two small teeth (probably incisors); in females both normally remain small and functionless but in males the left one grows fast and long, jutting out of the jaw. The function of the tusk has long been debated. As it is primarily a male trait, many think it must be involved somehow in sexual selection (differential mate choice), with females favouring more generously tusked males. However, other possible functions include as a (literal) ice-breaker in the Arctic seas Narwhals inhabit and even as a sophisticated sensory organ, capable of accurately determining water temperature and pressure. The tusk is indeed exceedingly well supplied with nerve endings but it seems odd that only males would get to reap the benefits.

---

## FASTEST AND SLOWEST HEARTBEATS

*Small hummingbirds' hearts can achieve an astounding 1,200 beats a minute when they are in active flight and small shrews rival this when they are running about. The slowest heartbeat of a warm-blooded animal is that of the Blue Whale, with just four to eight beats a minute, though crocodiles can slow theirs down to just two.*

---

## A LIGHT IN THE DARK

Deep-sea fishes are, by and large, an unprepossessing bunch. One of the most unattractive is the female Humpback Anglerfish (*Melanocetus johnsonii*), a lumpy, paunchy, front-heavy fish with its squashed visage dominated by a huge gaping maw packed with long, pointy teeth. In the gloom of the deep sea, though, no one is scrutinizing her face; instead all attention is on the glowing bobble on the end of a stalk of flesh that grows out of the fish's forehead. Attracted by the light, smaller fish swim close to the anglerfish and get snapped up in those unspeakable jaws. The light is generated by bacteria that live inside the bobble – they come from the surrounding seawater, and each of the other four *Melanocetus* species uses a different kind of bacteria. Males are much smaller, bobble-less and don't feed at all; they live only to supply their frightening womenfolk with sperm – more about that later.

## SOMETHING INSIDE SO STRONG

Most of us go out of our way to avoid standing on small mammals. To do so would surely be as psychologically upsetting for the human as it would be physically devastating for the small mammal. It must have been someone without such qualms who discovered that the Hero Shrew (*Scutisorex somereni*) of Africa can be stood upon by a 72kg human without coming to any harm. It weighs up to 90g, of which about 4 per cent (more than twice as much as similar-sized mammals) is its tremendously sturdy spinal column, which has a unique interlocking structure. Why this particular shrew species, which in other respects is not much different from all the other shrews, needs such solid internal scaffolding is not yet known (in other words, it's anyone's guess).

❦ ❦ ❦ ❦ ❦ ❦ ❦ ❦ ❦ ❦ ❦ ❦ ❦ ❦ ❦ ❦ ❦ ❦ ❦ ❦ ❦ ❦ ❦ ❦ ❦ ❦ ❦

## LARGEST PENIS

*Given that most birds don't have them at all, it's a bit of a surprise that the biggest penis by proportion to body size (among vertebrates) belongs to a duck. The Argentine Lake Duck (Oxyura vittata) has a 42.5cm 'manhood', all the more impressive when you note that the duck himself is only about 40cm long. In the invertebrate world, barnacles (infraclass Cirripedia) beat that easily, with penises 40 times longer than their bodies – essential if you want to mate with the barnacle next to you but neither of you can move.*

❦ ❦ ❦ ❦ ❦ ❦ ❦ ❦ ❦ ❦ ❦ ❦ ❦ ❦ ❦ ❦ ❦ ❦ ❦ ❦ ❦ ❦ ❦ ❦ ❦ ❦ ❦

## BABY'S GOT BACK

If possessing a backbone is a mark of bravery, the Slender Snipe Eel (*Nemichthys scolopaceus*) must be the most courageous fish in the sea. It has no fewer than 750 vertebrae, more than any other animal, giving its very slim, 1.5m body impressive flexibility. Its namesake, the Snipe (*Gallinago gallinago*), is a very long-billed wading bird, and the eel has a long 'beak' too, which it swishes from side to side to catch little sea creatures. One more oddity of this and the other snipe eels is that its anus is on its throat. Perhaps it's fortunate that eels can't cough.

## PORTION OF RIBS

Any hungry predator that decides to make a meal of a Chinhai Spiny Newt (*Echinotriton chinhaiensis*) may end up with more of a mouthful than it wanted. This Chinese amphibian is rather squat and slow-moving, and looks like easy prey. However, under the skin it has elongated, pointy-tipped ribs, and if a predator takes hold of it those rib tips break through the skin, piercing the predator's mouth. Not only that but the rib tips also pass through poison glands in the newt's skin, so when they puncture the predator's mouth they deliver an injection of toxins which causes pain and swelling. This species can potentially live for 20 years or more in the wild – plenty of time to put its poison-ribs defence to the test.

## A BIRD THAT'S NOT FOR THE TABLE

In Papua New Guinea, wild birds of various species are often on the menu for the humans who live in the forests. One group of birds, however, will not go down well at a Papua New Guinea dinner party. The pitohuis (genus *Pitohui*) are attractive and striking thrush-like birds with bold orange and black plumage and they are poisonous. This fact was made known to western scientists when an American ecology student was scratched by a pitohui he'd trapped in a mist net while studying forest birds in Papua New Guinea. On sucking the wounds left by the angry bird, he found his mouth went numb and tingly. The Papua New Guineans had, of course, long known about this and had dubbed the pitohuis 'rubbish birds' as a result. The toxins in their bodies are probably a result of eating certain beetles, and their colourful plumage may function as a warning. This would help predators build an association between their appearance and their inedibility and thus avoid hunting them.

## SOFT STEPPING

You probably thought you knew what a leg was. If you define a leg as something an animal uses to walk around with then that's fine but if you want to get any more specific than that things get complicated. The legs of velvet worms (phylum Onychophora) are particularly removed from what we think of as typical legs. They are not supported by bone or chitin (the hard stuff that insect exoskeletons are made of) or any other tough material but are just baggy outpouchings of the animal's soft skin whose rigidity is maintained by pressure from the movement of internal bodily fluids. Velvet worms have up to 43 pairs of these little, stumpy 'lobopods', each one tipped with a pair of claws to provide traction.

---

### LARGEST FLYING BIRDS

*The Wandering Albatross has a wingspan of 3.63m, considerably more than that of the heaviest flying bird (probably the Kori Bustard (Ardeotis kori) or Great Bustard (Otis tarda), both of which may reach 21kg). Just for completeness, the albatross weighs up to 13.8kg and the bustards' wingspan is about 2.5m. The tallest flyer is the Sarus Crane (Grus antigone), which may stand 1.8m tall.*

---

## CONFINED TO (SOME) CELLS

A human body contains something like 100 trillion cells (that's 10 with 14 noughts after it). Counting them all would take more time than anybody has to spare but if I counted mine and you counted yours the chances of us coming out with the exact same number are vanishingly small. Not so with rotifers. These squat, tiny (the biggest species reach 2mm), spiky-mouthed marine worms exhibit a property called eutely, which means that every adult has exactly the same number of cells in its body. Eutely occurs in several other microscopic animals, all of them with relatively modest total cell counts (rarely exceeding 1,000), though the actual size of each cell may vary.

## THE DEER-PIG

Huge canine teeth aren't just for carnivores. One of the other mammal groups that excel in this department is the pig family (family Suidae), and the toothiest pigs of all are the male babirusas (genus *Babyrousa*) of Indonesia. Their lower canines are impressive enough, growing upwards and back in a sweeping curve above the snout. However, it's the upper set that is really remarkable. They grow upwards out of the top of the snout, rather than the bottom, and break through the skin, growing in a similar backswept curve to the lower set. This means that none of a male babirusa's canine teeth are actually in his mouth. It also gives male babirusas an almost antlered appearance, and 'babirusa' means 'pig deer'. The theory is that the tusks help protect their eyes during tusk-on-tusk combat.

### BIGMOUTH STRIKES AGAIN

A pelican (family Pelecanidae) is noted for possessing a 'beak that can hold more than its belly can', both long and wide with a capacious pouch slung under the lower mandible. This bird has given its name to a similarly disproportionate fish, the Pelican Eel (*Eurypharynx pelecanoides*), which lives in deep seas and is as weird to behold as you might by now be expecting any deep-sea fish to be. It has a long body which attenuates to a very narrow, whippy tail, equipped with a light-emitting photophore at the tip. This enticing little blob of light is thought to serve as a lure for its crustacean prey, which are engulfed by the unseen yet colossal mouth when they get close enough. The mouth is many times wider than even the thickest part of the eel's body and its depth takes up a quarter of the eel's total length (with that thin, whippy tail accounting for more than half of what's left).

### DUCKS' TEETH

Birds don't have teeth. Those little enamelled nobbles are heavy for their size, and as ancient birds began to fly, natural selection strongly favoured the lightest individuals, so teeth disappeared and bird bills, made of lightweight keratin, became ever more diverse and versatile, to make up for the lack of teeth to grip, tear or crush their food. One group of birds does have

## LONGEST-LEGGED BIRD

*While the Ostrich (Struthio camelus) is the largest, tallest and heaviest bird, flamingos have the longest legs relative to body size in the world, with a group of smaller wading birds called (appropriately) stilts (genus Himantopus) coming a close second. Swifts, which cannot walk on land and spend most of their lives in flight, have the shortest.*

*So, what's your new girlfriend like?*

*Well, she's leggy...*

an approximation to teeth, though – the sawbilled ducks (genera *Mergus* and *Mergellus*). These diving ducks are fish-eaters, but while most fish-eating birds have dagger-like bills, sawbills have a kind of long, narrow version of a standard duck bill. The difference is inside: the inner edge of the bill is lined with little, sharp points like the teeth of a saw, ideal for gripping a slippery fish.

# CHAPTER 3

# SENSORY SENSATIONS

How often do we get told that our eyesight is rubbish in comparison with that of a hawk, our sense of smell useless compared with a dog, our hearing pathetic alongside that of a bat? Actually, humans don't have a bad array of sensory capabilities. We have better vision than dogs, a better sense of smell than a hawk and better... touch (probably) than bats, so we are reasonable all-rounders, but across the whole sweep of the animal world are sensory skills of all degrees and some animals possess extraordinary senses that we don't have at all. This chapter also looks at animal intelligence and what they do with all of that sensory data they have collected.

## DIRECTIONAL SMELLING

Ever wondered why snakes have forked tongues? It's not just to make them look extra scary but for the same reason that we have two eyes and ears – to give them stereo 'smell-o-vision' so they can better detect the presence of prey ... or danger. Snakes constantly flick their tongues in and out (without opening their jaws – there's a handy gap so they don't have to). While it's out, the tongue is gathering molecules of smelly chemicals from the air around it, just as our nostrils do. When the tongue is brought back in, the two forks fit into two special openings leading to the Jacobson's organ in the snake's mouth, which is full of chemoreceptive cells. If the left fork brings in more molecules of a particular smell than the right fork does, the snake knows the source of the smell is to its left and can home in on it – or avoid it – as appropriate.

## THE FISH THAT WEARS BIFOCALS

Lousy distance vision *and* rubbish close-up vision? No problem – bifocal glasses blend two kinds of lens so when you look up through the glass in the upper half of the frame you can see what's far away and looking down through the lower half lets you focus on the close-up stuff. But like many great ideas, animals had it first. Fish of the genus *Anableps* have two pupils in each eye, which enables them to swim at the surface and look through the air with the top half of the eye and simultaneously through the (optically very different) water with the bottom half.

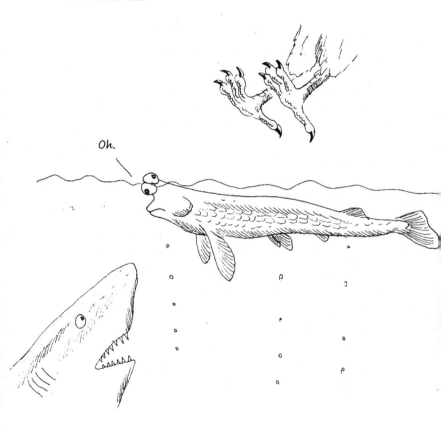

Oh.

## EYES AND STALKS

Those most otherworldly amphibians, the legless caecilians (order Gymnophiona), have some unique sensory features, most notably a pair of tiny tentacles close to their mouths. These unique organs are thought to be involved in smell and/or taste, but in two genera, *Scolecomorphus* and *Crotaphatrema*, they also have a role in sight. When these animals fully extend their tentacles, their eyes move out of their usual position in the skull and into the base of the tentacles, which has no pigment so light can reach the eyes. Why? The eyes are, in their normal position, tucked under skull bone, making the animal pretty much blind. No big deal for an animal that lives underground; most caecilians can't see much and some have no eyes at all. However, it seems possible that these particular caecilians can choose to see (or at least detect light) more effectively when they push out their tentacles.

### MOST SENSITIVE SENSE OF SMELL

*This probably belongs to the bears, which have far more sensitive noses than the most competent bloodhound. However, males of some moths are incredibly sensitive to specific chemicals (those associated with female moths) and can detect a single molecule of the female's pheromone.*

## EARS FALSE AND REAL

Some owls have feathery tufts on their heads that look like ears. They're not though; they're just feathery tufts – perhaps for shape camouflage, or maybe to make the owl face resemble that of a cat and thus seem scarier to would-be predators and rivals. The owl's real ears have no external structure – just holes in the skin on the sides of the head, as with all birds. Find a cooperative owl and gently part the feathers there if you want to see its ear-holes. The facial disk of an owl helps channel sound into these ear-holes, and the owl, like us, can find the source of a sound according to whether the left or right ear hears it first. Unlike us, some owl species have asymmetrically placed inner ears, one higher than the other, to help the owl accurately pinpoint the source of a sound coming from directly below (or indeed above). As if it were needed, one more demonstration of this night hunter's superb hearing comes from its brain, in which the 'hearing centre' has up to three times as many brain cells as you'd find in a crow.

*I said,*
ARE THESE
REAL EARS?

## FEELING HOT, HOT, HOT

The colours we humans can see form a section of the electromagnetic spectrum that we call 'visible light'. The wavelengths that are just longer than this section are infrared and we can't see them but we perceive them as heat when they hit our skin. Pit vipers (family Crotalinae) have a particular interest in detecting heat – specifically that emitted from the body of a nearby tasty rodent or other mammalian prey item – and to help them do so they have special infrared-sensitive organs on their heads. Under and in front of their eyes they have what looks like an elongated extra nostril on each side, a 'loreal pit', in which is a structurally complex and highly sensitive 'pit organ' that detects infrared radiation and enables the snake to locate the source of the heat accurately, before eating it.

## HALF AN EYE

Charles Darwin is a much-quoted guy. Take this one from 1872: 'To suppose that the eye, with all its inimitable contrivances for adjusting the focus to different distances, for admitting different amounts of light, and for the correction of spherical and chromatic aberration, could have been formed by natural selection, seems, I freely confess, absurd in the highest possible degree.' Taken out of context (as it often is) it sounds like he is dismissing his own theory of evolution by natural selection. However, he goes on to explain that numerous small improvements, each affording some advantage and each inherited by the next generation, could (given enough time) quite feasibly produce a refined modern vertebrate eye from the humblest beginnings. The eye of the nautilus (family Nautilidae), a mollusc, is a real-life representation of one of the 'intermediate' stages. It has no lens and is just a pit with a tiny aperture to admit light, like a pinhole camera, but affords some vision so is clearly better for the nautilus than no eye at all.

## ENOUGH TO MAKE YOUR EYES BLEED

Prepare for a shock if you are going to harass a horned lizard (genus *Phrynosoma*). If they are feeling really threatened, these spiky-headed reptiles from North America can shoot blood from their eye-sockets; it's unclear whether the would-be predator is supposed to be repelled by this unusual action or just feel so sorry for them that the urge to eat them disappears. The blood is generated by exploding blood vessels in the eyes and can travel up to 1.2m. It is obviously not especially pleasant for the lizard itself, which is why it is a last-ditch measure if its previous tactics of camouflage and then threat displays have failed.

## SOUNDS FROM THE DEEP

Studying the sensory capabilities of deep-sea fish is beyond our means at the moment, as such fish are adapted to live under the intense pressure of very deep water and quickly die if brought to the surface for a hearing test. Examination of their anatomy has revealed that some species may well possess extraordinarily acute hearing, as they show strange structures such as long, bony stalks projecting from their otoliths (ear 'stones' which help conduct sound) and also a rigid inner ear, which may help conduct vibrations from the swim bladder: a structure used for buoyancy, the swim bladder may also help to amplify sound waves.

## IS THERE AN ECHO IN HERE?

Sonar is a fantastic human invention whereby sound is used to locate stuff, by detecting the echoes produced when sound waves bounce off an object. Like so many other great human inventions it has been around in the animal world for millennia – both bats and dolphins use echolocation to find their way around their respective aerial and watery worlds, emitting a constant stream of squeaks or clicks as they go. That's why, if a bat gets into your room, it will probably not collide with anything and the same is probably true of a dolphin somehow getting stuck in a swimming pool party in a power cut.

## SCENT OF A MOTH

Imagine you're a female Emperor Moth (*Pavonia pavonia*), fully formed in your cocoon and ready to come out and see the world. You spent a long summer as a caterpillar then a long winter pupating and now you're ready to spread your brand new wings, so you start struggling out of your cocoon. What you don't know is that there's a welcome party out there – dozens of male Emperor Moths, attracted from up to 10km away by the aroma of the pheromones you're unwittingly releasing. Before you've even fully emerged and well before your wings have expanded enough for flight, one of those eager males will have won the struggle to mate with you. Is it any wonder that entomologists describe female Emperor Moths as 'rather sluggish'?

*I think I'll just stay in here...*

## HAWK-EYE

Or, in this case, Falcon-eye. At a falconry demonstration, you may see the falconer showing off his birds' amazingly acute eyesight with this trick. The falcon is sent off from the fist and climbs high in the sky, until it is just a speck to the onlookers. As it continues to rise, the beeps from its radio transmitter get further and further apart. Soon it is invisibly high, though the falconer's receiver continues to beep. Then the falconer moves his hand slightly, towards the bag he's carrying that contains a meaty treat for the falcon. At this tiny movement, the radio beeps start to speed up. Even though no one on the ground can see the bird, the bird can see that movement and starts to descend. Birds of prey like this don't have magnified vision, just extremely high acuity. Think of it as the difference between looking at a low- versus high-resolution image.

### BEST NIGHT VISION

*The likely winner in this category is one or other of the most nocturnal of the owls, which can spot prey over impressive distances in what to us would be total darkness. However, owls' close-up vision is poor, which is perhaps why they are often depicted wearing reading glasses.*

## GRAVITY FOR BIRDS

Thanks to artists like M.C. Escher and now the miracle that is Photoshop, we can all enjoy 'impossible' images which look real but can't be, because they defy the laws of physics. Scientists investigating what animals make of such impossible images showed their subjects gravity-defying images, such as eggs floating in mid-air, alongside perfectly normal and feasible images. Rather surprisingly, they found that Rooks (*Corvus frugilegus*) were most taken aback by the 'impossible' pictures, spending much longer scrutinizing them than they did the ordinary images. Chimpanzees (*Pan troglodytes*), on the other hand, showed no particular interest in the gravity-defying pictures. It seems bizarre to us that a type of crow would be cleverer than a great ape but there's no doubt that, among birds, the Rook is one of the smartest.

## BIN-BUSTERS

Many animals have learned that black bin bags often contain tasty titbits. Depending where you live you may suffer bag depredations from foxes, Raccoons, gulls, crows or domestic cats. However, a group of clever Rooks (*Corvus frugilegus*) frequenting a certain UK service station have learned a clever way to get at bin bags that are still inside public litter bins, without taking the risk of actually jumping inside. They sit on the bin edge and use their bills to hoick up a fold of bin bag. This they secure with their feet before grabbing the next fold and so on, eventually bringing the contents within reach.

## THE WATER SMELLS LOVELY

Shrews (family Soricidae) are very scent-oriented animals, as is evident by their tiny eyes, insignificant ears and long, pointy noses. Some shrews are part-time aquatic animals, living close to rivers and pools and frequently swimming, diving and hunting underwater. They are not so well adapted to watery life that they don't still need to breathe through their noses, which makes it difficult for them to use their favourite sense underwater, but evolution has found a way. To smell its underwater surroundings, a water shrew exhales an air bubble underwater. The air immediately picks up nearby smells, so when the shrew swiftly inhales it again, it can smell any aquatic prey that happens to be around.

## EYELESS SIGHT, EARLESS HEARING

The humble Common Earthworm (*Lumbricus terrestris*) doesn't seem, on first inspection, to be overly endowed in the sensory department. Even without recognizable eyes and ears, though, this animal and its relatives are still able to perceive light and sound. It has simple light-sensitive organs in its first two body segments and can detect sound through vibrations. Because they come to the earth's surface to mate, Common Earthworms need to detect light to help find their way there. Because they need it to be raining when they come up (so that they and the soil are wet enough) they need to 'hear' rain falling on the soil's surface. When you see a gull in a field doing a little on-the-spot, 'Riverdance'-style jig, it's trying to recreate the sound of falling rain to trick the worms into coming up.

Banging party
on the surface!

## FURTHEST-CARRYING ANIMAL SOUND

*Big animal, big voice. Blue Whales' (Balaenoptera musculus) calls carry hundreds of kilometres and hit an impressive 188 decibels. Many tropical animals have far-carrying contact calls as it's easier to be heard than seen in dense rainforests; howler monkey (genus Alouatta) howls carry 3km or more across the South and Central American jungles.*

## SNEAKY ASSASSIN

Insects are not generally considered especially intelligent, which makes the hunting behaviour of a certain assassin bug, *Salyavata variegate*, all the more sinister. The bug preys on termites (order Isoptera) and gets close to their nests by festooning itself with discarded nest material, so it does not give itself away by having an inappropriate smell. After it has found, captured and sucked dry its first victim, it attracts another by waving the first one's corpse around at the nest entrance. This attracts more termites from within the nest, keen to investigate and perhaps 'clean up' the remains of their fallen comrade. The bug may bump off 35 termites in a single visit.

## TOO LOUD TO HEAR

There is a theory around that the decline of House Sparrows (*Passer domesticus*) in city centres is because traffic noise is now so overwhelming that the birds can't hear each other's courtship calls. If this is the case, perhaps the sparrows need to go down the same route as Angel's Madagascar Frog (*Boehmantis microtympanum*). These sizeable frogs inhabit fast-flowing streams in the uplands, where there is a constant deafening roar of rushing water. While most frogs are quite vocal animals, it's thought that this little-known species may not call at all, as it has very reduced and perhaps functionless eardrums. If all you can ever hear is the sound of ceaseless torrents of water, perhaps after many millennia you start physically tuning it out.

## EXPANDING THE SPECTRUM

The mantis shrimp version of our familiar electromagnetic radiation chart would look very different from ours. For us, visible light is a very narrow band, bordered by the much wider bands of infrared on one side and ultraviolet on the other. Mantis shrimps' visible band would be many times wider, as they can see both infrared and ultraviolet light. These strange, colourful and elegant sea crustaceans possess 16 different types of colour receptor in their eyes (humans have three – though see 'Four colours in her eyes', on page 88, for a few that don't), so while they look colourful to us they probably look much more so to each other. They can also see circular polarized light (that's light waves that are travelling on a single plane, rather than through all planes like normal light – to our eyes it looks

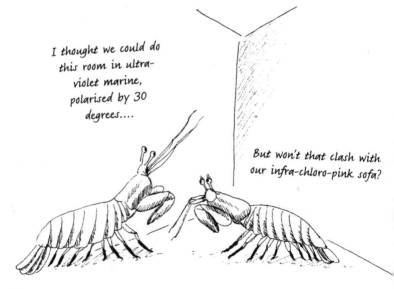

like light glare). The three sections that each (independently moveable) eye is divided into mean that mantis shrimps also possess trinocular vision – in each eye.

---

## LARGEST EARS

*The African Bush Elephant (Loxodonta africana) has the largest external ears of any animal, though they are the size they are to help cool the animal down as well as to enhance its hearing.*

---

## BEATING THE BAT

Echolocation is the primary means by which bats find their prey, and the top bat prey is moths. However, moths have not taken this treatment lying down. A variety of ways to foil hunting bats has evolved among various moth lineages. The tiger moth *Bertholdia trigona* sends out bursts of clicking sounds of its own, which confuses the bats' echolocation system and helps protect the moth from attack. It produces its clicks by the contraction of organs called tymbals on its abdomen.

## LASHINGS OF LASHES

Eyelashes are there to help shade the eyes and protect them from dust so it's no surprise that we see the longest ones in animals that live in exposed and sunny places. Giraffes are famously well equipped in the lash department, as are camels. Birds don't have eyelashes as such, not possessing body hair, but some species have modified feathers over their eyes which look and function just like mammalian eyelashes. The Secretarybird (*Sagittarius serpentarius*) and the ground-hornbills (genus *Bucorvus*) are both large, mainly ground-dwelling savannah species which boast impressive pseudolashes. The Eyelash Viper (*Bothriechis schlegelii*) has scales over its eyes that look a little like lashes but don't move when the snake blinks – because snakes don't blink. So they don't function like proper lashes but are instead thought to form part of its camouflage.

## MELON-FEATURES

Many bats have disproportionately large ears, appropriate to their sound-led lifestyle. In toothed whales and dolphins, the other famous echolocators, there is a separate organ called the 'melon' which is (probably) involved in echolocation. The melon is found in the forehead and is composed of various fatty materials, which have been shown to conduct sound waves at different rates. It is also responsible for giving dolphins and toothed whales that bulging-browed look that we humans find so cute.

## TELL-TALE TRAIL

If you've ever watched a Kestrel (*Falco tinnunculus*) hovering motionless high over a field, you may have marvelled at its ability to spot a tiny vole moving in the long grass from way up there. Kestrels, however, have the ability to see something that we probably couldn't spot even at point-blank range – the trail of urine droplets that voles and other small rodents leave behind as they move around. Ultraviolet light highlights the fresh pee trail, giving the Kestrel a clear sign of where to target its search for the vole itself.

## BRAIN COMPASS

It's one of the greatest mysteries of nature. A young Swallow (*Hirundo rustica*) sets off on its first migration and flies all the way from England to sub-Saharan Africa. Next spring, it flies back again, and sometime in April breezes into the very village it was born in. How does it find its way? How does it adjust for the inevitable problems en route that throw it off course?

Studies have shown that migrating birds use a whole range of visual cues to help them navigate but one helpful extra attribute they have is the ability to detect the Earth's magnetic field. How? An area in their upper bills containing an iron-based compound called magnetite is probably involved; there is also an eye pigment in birds which responds to magnetic fields.

Um, is this the North Pole?

## IT'S HAMMER-TIME

Picture a strange animal head. Some of you will probably have come up with that of a hammerhead shark (genus *Sphyrna*), especially given the cunning hint in the heading. These bizarre sharks have flattened, wide heads with eyes set at the far corners. The head is quite hydrodynamic in its own way, being shaped a bit like an aerofoil. But what's the point of having the eyes so far apart? Despite the distance between them, the orientation of the eyes means the two visual fields have considerable overlap, giving the shark exceptional binocular vision and therefore great depth perception, and no significant blind spots in front (behind is, of course, another matter).

## CRUSHED NUTS

We've already seen how bright Rooks (*Corvus frugilegus*) can be. Over in Japan, Carrion Crows (*Corvus corone*) have learned an equally clever trick. At a certain busy crossroads by a university campus, the crows collect walnuts from the walnut trees that line the streets and, when the traffic is stationary at the lights, they place their nuts on the road then retreat. The cars move off in due course, running over the nuts and breaking the shells. Next time the lights change and the cars stop, the crows fly down and eat up the walnut fragments. Crows in captivity have been shown to be capable of elaborate tool use to access food but it's particularly impressive to see them effectively using tools as large and formidable as Hondas, Subarus and Mitsubishis.

Why did I ever say I was good at using tools?

## CLEVER CEPHALOPODS

It's long been suspected that octopuses and squids (class Cephalopoda) are a cut above other squishy sea animals when it comes to intelligence. Analysing their intelligence is difficult for us, as their world is so radically different from what's familiar ground for humans. However, in 2009 scientists discovered that the Veined Octopus (*Amphioctopus marginatus*) demonstrates one of the benchmarks of superior intelligence – tool use. It lives in shallow tropical Pacific waters, where halved coconut shells discarded by people are readily found on the sea bed. The octopus will use a single shell-half to hide underneath, but it prefers to collect a pair of shells and arrange them into a clam-shaped protective fortress, within which it hides.

## EYES ON THE MOVE

Most of us have seen dead flatfish (order Pleuronectiformes) like plaice or soles on the fishmonger's ice and may have noticed their weird eyes. Nearly all vertebrates have faces that are vertically symmetrical, so the asymmetrical flatfish eyes, both on the same side of its head, look very strange to us. How they get that way is even stranger. The young fish fry starts off with its eyes in the conventional places, one on each side of its head. As the fish grows and its body starts to flatten, one eye sets off on a journey to join the other one. Both look upwards – handy for a fish that spends its life lying on the sea bed – and the asymmetry and thus lack of a familiar 'fish-face' may help disguise the fish from predators.

## MAGNETIC PERSONALITIES

Birds aren't the only ones with magnetoception. It's been observed in many other groups, even in humans (to a very limited extent). The cartilaginous fish (including rays and sharks) have organs in their heads called ampullae of Lorenzini, which detect electromagnetic fields. Crocodiles use their magnetoception to navigate and can return to their home ranges even after being relocated many miles away; certain 'problem crocs' living in residential areas have been fitted with magnets after relocation to prevent them returning.

## TASTY FEET

How does a mother butterfly know which plant to lay her eggs on? Most caterpillars are only able to feed from one or a few different plant species so it's important mum gets it right. She identifies the correct plant by taste – conveniently, her taste receptors are on her feet. They are sensitive enough to pick up the unique signature chemicals from the plant on contact. Oddly, despite this ability, butterflies of a few species just drop their eggs in flight while traversing what looks like a suitable area of vegetation.

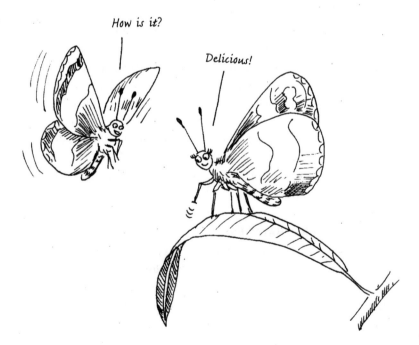

## VISION IN THE EGG

Cuttlefish are sea molluscs, related to octopuses. They have very developed eyes, which can detect polarized light and thus see enhanced levels of light contrast. They also have two foveas (the point of sharpest focus on the eye's retina) – one to see in front of them and the other behind. Cuttlefish eyes are well developed and apparently well used even before the baby cuttlefish hatches from its egg; experiments have shown that the babies will preferentially go after types of prey that they 'saw' prior to hatching.

### GREATEST HEARING RANGE

*Dolphins can hear an impressive range of frequencies, from 200 to 150,000Hz, but some species of moths beat them to the top end, with a range of 1,000 to 240,000Hz.*

## LOOK AT IT THIS WAY

The ability to see something – anything – can be as simple as a light-detecting organelle inside a single-celled *Paramecium* or as complex as the extraordinarily acute eyes of a bird of prey. As eyes go, those of vertebrate animals are pretty good, but they possess a 'design flaw' which doesn't make much sense – the nerves in the eye are in front of the light-detecting cells of the retina, and where those nerves join up and go through the retina on their way to the brain, there is a blind spot in our vision. Eye movement and creative input from our brains means we hardly ever notice it. However, octopuses' (order Octopoda) eyes evolved via a different pathway, and their retinas and nerves are the 'right way round', with light detectors in front of nerves and no blind spot.

## MOONSTRUCK

Ever watched a moth throwing itself at a lamp and thought 'what an idiot'? Don't be too hard on the poor thing. Night-flying moths and other insects are thought to navigate by maintaining a position relative to the moon, which was, until recently, the only significant light source in the night sky. Because the moon is so far away, the moth will go in a straight line if it keeps the moon in the same point in its visual field. Our artificial lights, however, are of course much closer, and when the moth tries to do the same thing with your outside lamp it just goes round and round in tight circles.

*I must be nearly in orbit by now.*

## FOUR COLOURS IN HER EYES

The bog-standard human retina contains three types of colour-detecting cone cell, one for red light, one for green and one for blue. All of the rest of the colours in our visible light spectrum can be made up of combinations of red, green and blue. Most birds have four kinds of cone cells – the same three as us plus another for ultraviolet light, so while we are trichromats ('three-colour things'), birds are tetrachromats ('four-colour things'). However, there may be a handful of tetrachromats among the human population. Two possible candidates – both English women – have been identified who show enhanced colour differentiation skills and may possess a fourth kind of cone, not for ultraviolet light but for wavelengths midway between red and green. Because the genes for two of the three cone pigments reside on the human X chromosome, tetrachromy in humans is only likely to be observed in women (with their two X chromosomes) and could theoretically affect some 3 per cent of the female population.

## SYNAESTHESIA

While our eyes, ears, skin, tongue and nose take in sensory information from the world around us, it's our brains that make sense of it for us. Some people report that sensory input of one kind is experienced as if it was a different kind of input; for example, they experience sounds as colours or flavours. Until we learn to talk to the animals, we won't know whether other species besides ourselves experience these sensory mix-ups. Perhaps 'cross-overs' would be a better term than 'mix-ups'; it's been theorized that synaesthetes improve their ability to remember things by their involuntary mental trick of forming multiple associations for the same stimulus.

## HEAR YOU LATER, ALLIGATOR

We don't tend to think of reptiles as a very vocal bunch. Snakes hiss, geckos squeak but many other species are almost silent. Making up for this, the American Alligator (*Alligator mississippiensis*) is a great conversationalist, with a wide repertoire of noises, from coughs, bellows and grunts to a startlingly lion-like roaring, which can be heard 150m away. It accomplishes all of this despite being without any vocal cords; instead, the sound is generated by breathing in a big lungful of air and then huffing it out again at high speed.

## GOOD (AND BAD) VIBRATIONS

One reason you don't often see snakes when you're out and about in good snake habitat is that they can hear you coming, even if you keep the whistling, stomping and cheery conversation to a minimum. Snakes hear with their whole bodies, picking up ground vibrations through their skin and conducting those vibrations via their skeletons to the jawbones, which transfer the vibrations to the inner ears. Because so many snakes are ambush hunters, being exquisitely sensitive to other animals moving around in their vicinity is a vital skill and it also gives them plenty of advance notice when an eager snake-watcher is approaching.

## SIDEWAYS GLANCE

Woodcocks (genus *Scolopax*) are very beautiful but slightly odd-looking birds. It's something about the look of their faces, specifically the position of their eyes – just that bit further back on their heads than expected. In fact, even if you stand directly behind a Woodcock, you can still see its eyes – and it can still see you. Most birds have eyes set on the sides of their heads to give them a good all-round view, rather than forward-facing eyes for good binocular vision and improved depth perception. Woodcocks, with their oddly placed eyes, have the largest visual field of any bird, spanning the full 360 degrees.

### LARGEST EYES

*An adult Colossal Squid (Mesonychoteuthis hamiltoni) has eyes as large as the proverbial dinner plate, measuring nearly 30cm across. They are probably the largest of any animal, though because very few specimens of this species and the various giant squids (genus Architeuthis) have been examined, it's hard to be certain. The eyes of the Vampire Squid (Vampyroteuthis infernalis) are the largest relative to body size.*

## SENSITIVE NOSES

Since the nose is the most protuberant part of most mammals' faces and the bit most likely to be thrust first into new, interesting and potentially dangerous situations, it's not really surprising that noses are quite sensitive to touch. This is dramatically obvious in the case of the Star-nosed Mole (*Condylura cristata*), whose snout is tipped with a circle of little, pink, tentacle-like protrusions. The 22 highly mobile appendages (11 per nostril) are bountifully equipped with touch sensors, which enable the mole to detect by touch even the smallest potential prey items.

*Stupid tentacles.*

## CHAPTER 4

# MARVELLOUS MIGRATIONS

At the time of writing, the UK is battling through one of the worst winters for decades and it's easy to feel envious of the birds that left our shores months ago to spend winter in the southern hemisphere. Migratory journeys are immensely costly in terms of energy consumption and there are many risks on the way, but for some species they are obviously worthwhile for a winter of (relatively) easy living. Or, to look at it from a less northern-centric perspective, it's worth these birds' while to fly north in spring and take advantage of our long summers to breed, rather than remain south of the equator and compete with the many resident birds there for nesting and food resources. Some animals undertake regular seasonal migrations; others do it just once or twice in a lifetime. Some travel only when it's a necessity, while for others the whole of their lifetime is one big journey. Birds aren't the only great travellers in the animal world, of course, and one animal's quick and effortless jaunt may be another's epic voyage – it's all a question of scale.

### AN AMERICAN DRAGON IN CORNWALL

Every autumn, hundreds of birdwatchers travel to Cornwall and the Scilly Isles in the hope that their visit will coincide with that of one or more 'vagrant' birds from North America, blown off course across the Atlantic as they migrate south. An Atlantic crossing, even if it is wind-assisted, seems an amazing feat for a small bird, so how much more amazing a journey is it for an insect? Yet several insect species have made the crossing, including the Green Darner dragonfly (*Anax junius*). Several individuals of this species made it across in 1998 and at least one survived for more than a week, suggesting it was none the worse for its incredible journey.

I don't think we're in Kansas any more...

## NOT SO SUICIDAL

Just as the Dodo represents extinction, so the lemming represents suicide. While the Dodo is unquestionably extinct, lemmings do not in fact suffer the urge to end their lives. The myth comes from the mass migrations of the Norway Lemming (*Lemmus lemmus*), a small rodent which, in common with other small rodents, is very good at making babies. If weather conditions are particularly conducive to lemming baby-making activity, the population will go through the roof and suddenly there are far too many lemmings and not enough for them to eat. Therefore, a mass migration (which to the untutored eye looks like a mass panic) to new habitat will occur, and in the chaos many will inevitably fall into rivers or otherwise meet their ends but they don't do it on purpose.

## FOLLOWING THE FEAST

Most birds of prey in the UK are present all year round. One that isn't is the Hobby (*Falco subbuteo*), a highly skilled aerial hunter. In summer, it hunts a lot of large insects, especially dragonflies. Come autumn, dragonfly numbers dwindle and Hobbies switch to larger prey, particularly small birds. Being one of the few predators that's fast enough and agile enough to catch swallows and martins, Hobbies take full advantage of the pre-migratory congregations of these birds, and when the swallows and martins set off to migrate, so do the Hobbies, travelling in convenient proximity to their prey all the way to the wintering grounds.

The trouble with these long-haul flights is the food's so monotonous...

## LONGEST MIGRATION

*Satellite tagging has recently revealed that the longest migration on earth is that undertaken by the Sooty Shearwater (Puffinus griseus), a long-winged (unsurprisingly) seabird. It flies 74,000km a year in a curious figure-of-eight pattern across the Pacific Ocean.*

## LADIES' DAY

Some animals habitually undertake seasonal migrations no matter what. Others will only travel if something happens to give them a push – exceptional weather conditions, a shortage of food or perhaps a very successful breeding season, resulting in overpopulation and consequent depletion of local resources. In 2009, Painted Lady butterflies (*Vanessa cardui*) in Morocco had an exceptionally successful year, with the result that a huge northward migration took place. Most years some Painted Ladies reach the UK but in 2009 they vastly outnumbered our resident butterfly species. By late May they were making landfall in England in their thousands, with some 18,000 individuals coming in at north Norfolk in a single day. A new generation of butterflies born in the UK headed back south as autumn approached.

## HOMING INSTINCT

We've all seen TV footage of salmon leaping determinedly upriver, over boulders, up waterfalls and (in North America) sometimes into the cheerfully agape mouths of Grizzly Bears (*Ursus arctos*). Atlantic Salmon (*Salmo salar*) in Britain swim up to cold northern rivers in the uplands to spawn in November and most of them promptly die straight afterwards. Meanwhile, their eggs hatch in spring and the fry spend two years eating whatever drifts past before they are ready to migrate. Then it's off downriver until they reach the sea, their body chemistry changing on the way to adapt to living in salt rather than fresh water. After another two years or so they are ready to spawn and head inland for the perilous upriver journey that will end (after an ecstatic spawn-fest) in their deaths, in the very spot of river where they were born.

*Oh, for goodness sake... I TOLD you we should go the long way!*

## MAKING TRACKS

Early British naturalists didn't know that many birds flew south for the winter and came up with a variety of explanations for their disappearance, including the idea that Redstarts (*Phoenicurus phoenicurus*) mutated into Robins (*Erithacus rubecula*) and that Swallows (*Hirundo rustica*) whiled away the winter asleep in the mud at the bottom of ponds. We still don't

know where all birds go on their migrations but recent
advances in satellite tracking technology are helping to fill in
the gaps. Satellite tags fitted to three Northern Bald Ibises
(*Geronticus eremita*) at their nests in Syria revealed that this
critically endangered bird winters in Ethiopia, even though
there have been no confirmed sightings of the species in that
country for some 30 years.

## WHALE AWAY

Just like birds on land, some sea animals perform an annual
north–south migration to take advantage of the best times of
year in both hemispheres. The greatest undersea traveller is the
Humpback Whale (*Megaptera novaeangliae*), which spends its
summer feeding up in northern waters but heads south to mate
and bear its young in winter. Some populations travel as far as
8,700km each way, making the northward journey on an
almost empty stomach.

## NOMAD BUTTERFLY

One of the rarest butterflies in the UK is the Monarch (*Danaus
plexippus*), which occasionally accidentally crosses the Atlantic
from North America and usually causes a stir when it is found
here, thanks to its spectacular size and dramatic black, orange
and white colour scheme. In the Americas the species is famous
and much-loved for its extraordinary mass migrations and the
'relay race' of new generations that complete them. At the end
of summer the population heads south to the southern states
and Mexico, where they overwinter, often densely carpeting
trees in their favoured hibernation spots. Come spring they
return north, with the original butterflies breeding and dying
en route, being replaced by a new generation. In total, there
are three or four generations a year – all born during the
northward journey except the final one, which carries out the
southward migration.

## LONGEST NON-STOP FLIGHT

*As we'll see later, the Bar-tailed Godwit flies further than any other in one go. One tagged bird has the official record with her epic 11,680km, nine-day trip from Alaska to New Zealand.*

## GREAT BIG CONVOY

When a population of spiny lobsters (family Palinuridae) decide to move to a new part of the sea bed, they do it all together. Although they are not particularly social in their day-to-day lives, they keep in close contact when travelling, moving in long, single-file lines, with each lobster staying within touching distance of the one in front. The journey is necessitated when the lobsters' shallow habitat becomes too cold and the waters too disturbed for them, so they move on to pastures new (and deeper). Why they do it en masse in such an organized way is unclear, as each lobster possesses exceptionally good navigational skills and so would be quite capable of finding its way by itself.

## ALL THIS IS MINE

Most non-migratory mammals have a home range – an area within which they live and do not stray beyond. This is typically (and predictably) smaller for small mammals, bigger for the large ones. However, the type of habitat also plays a part, in particular, how its resources are distributed. Polar Bears (*Ursus maritimus*) often have to travel great distances to find their prey and consequently their home ranges can be huge – in excess of 350,000km$^2$ in some cases. When a young Polar Bear is all grown up and ready to find its own home range, it may have to walk 1,000km away from its mother to establish a home range of its own.

## ENDLESS SUMMER

In Earth's polar regions, summer is uninterrupted daylight and winter 24-hour darkness. So any animal that opts to spend the northern summer in the Arctic Circle and the southern summer in Antarctica will get to enjoy near-permanent daylight, if not necessarily the highest temperatures. The graceful and noisy Arctic Tern (*Sterna paradisaea*) travels up to 38,624km every year, one of the longest migrations of all animals, in its pole-to-pole trip. The most northerly Arctic Tern colonies lie well within the Arctic Circle, as far up as the north of Greenland, and in winter (the southern summer) they can be seen feeding around the retreating edge of the Antarctic ice. Being seabirds they can stop for a rest on calm water and can fish as they go, so their migration doesn't count as the longest non-stop flight.

Time for your bedtime story. 'It was a dark and stormy night...'

What's 'dark'? And what's a 'night'?

## FILLING THE TANK

Come autumn, if you go for a countryside walk you may notice lots of birds in the hedgerows, methodically eating berry after berry. Chances are that they are migratory species which are preparing to set off soon for their long journey. During the joyous period of overeating, a Garden Warbler (*Sylvia borin*) can increase its bodyweight by 10 per cent every day, ending up twice as heavy as it was before the feasting began. These substantial fat stores will help it to survive its 2,500km migration from northern Europe to central or southern Africa and cut down the amount of refuelling it needs to do en route.

## RIVERDANCE

The Blue Wildebeest (*Connochaetes taurinus*) is one of those unfortunate animals that we know best from seeing it being eaten by other animals in wildlife documentaries. When the dry season arrives in the Serengeti, the wildebeests must travel to upland areas to find fresh grazing, and the journey often involves a river crossing. Ignoring the Nile Crocodiles

(*Crocodylus niloticus*) lurking in the water and the wildlife film-makers crouched up on the banks, the wildebeests storm across the mighty Mara river by the thousand, supposedly using 'swarm intelligence' to find the quickest and safest route across the deep water and up the slippery bank. Inevitably an unlucky few drown or are seized by crocs but the vast majority gets across safely.

## PIONEERS

Back in 1956, a momentous ornithological event occurred – the first ever UK breeding of Collared Doves (*Streptopelia decaocto*). Since many of us could today go to the window and see a few Collared Doves right now (I can hear one cooing on the roof as I write), it's amazing to reflect how well they have done in so short a time. Before the 20th century, these attractive birds lived mainly in Asia. The agricultural revolution, while bad news for a lot of wildlife, was an absolute gift to these grain-eating, human-tolerating birds, and they followed its sweep across Europe, colonizing country after country. While the species' spread across Europe has been natural, it has been introduced by people to North America, where it is carrying out a similarly comprehensive colonization.

## LOST AT SEA

In 2008, the Royal Society for the Protection of Birds fitted satellite trackers to two young Ospreys (*Pandion haliaetus*) hatched that year on the Loch Garten RSPB reserve, to observe the migratory routes taken by these first-time travellers. One chick made it to traditional Osprey wintering grounds in West Africa but the other took a wrong turn and struck out west from south-east England along the English Channel on 26 September, soon finding himself out over the Atlantic. From then on, his fate was almost inevitable as Ospreys can't swim and need land on which to eat the fish they catch. However, before he finally ran out of steam and ditched into the sea, he flew on non-stop in the wrong direction for an astonishing four days, covering nearly 2,500km.

---

### HIGHEST INSECT FLIER

*It's the Globe Skimmer dragonfly (Pantala flavescens), which has been seen cruising at 6,900m above sea level in the Himalayas, no doubt on its way to somewhere exotic.*

---

## SETTLING DOWN

Think of an animal that doesn't move and you're likely to come up with something like a barnacle (crustaceans of the infraclass Cirripedia), which is firmly attached to a rock or other sea-covered object and stays there forever. However, the barnacles you see clustered all over the struts of the pier were once freely swimming animals. Fully grown larval barnacles or cyprids look like chubby little shrimps and swim around, sometimes for weeks, in search of somewhere to set up home for the rest of their lives. This is often a place that already has a colony of barnacles, hence their tendency to form dense clusters. Once attached, the cyprid forms the hard white plates that form the familiar casing of an adult barnacle.

## A PLANT FOR ALL SEASONS

Anyone who dismisses moths as brown and boring needs to take a look at the gorgeous Madagascar Sunset Moth (*Chrysiridia rhipheus*), which, to be fair, looks very like a colourful swallowtail-type butterfly. Endemic to the island of Madagascar, this species lays its eggs on four plants of the genus *Omphalea*. The four plants grow on different parts of the island, with three on the west coast and one on the east. The eastern species is the only one that is evergreen and therefore in a state eatable by caterpillars throughout the year. To exploit this, the moths migrate between the east and west coasts of the island, using the eastern *Omphalea* species when the other three are unavailable.

## STRAIT AND NARROW

Birds migrating between Europe and Africa often try to keep their sea crossings as short as possible. This is especially important for large, soaring birds, which use rising air currents (thermals) to gain height effortlessly; thermals don't happen over the sea so flying long distances over open water requires flapping, which uses up more energy. The Strait of Gibraltar provides a sea crossing distance of just 14km, so many thousands of raptors and storks take this path on their southern journeys. The birds use thermals at the land's edge to gain as much height as they can then glide across the Strait, losing

A little help?

altitude as they go. This provides an amazing spectacle for birdwatchers in Gibraltar in spring, as birds have often dropped down close to eye level by the time they have crossed the Strait.

## BRAND NEW ISLAND

An undersea volcanic eruption in 1963 produced a new island off the southern coast of Iceland. Since its appearance, the island of Surtsey has proved a fascinating case study for how animals travel to and colonize new islands. Continued volcanic activity over three and a half years resulted in a roughly $0.3km^2$ island of volcanic rock. By 1970, mosses, lichens and vascular plants had all arrived, courtesy of wind-borne seeds or spores. Flying insects were found from 1964, while in 1974 a large chunk of dislodged grass containing over 650 species of land invertebrates was washed up. Seals first bred in 1983, while the rocky shore soon teemed with intertidal life. A gull colony became established in 1984, providing guano that helped the plants to thrive; more than a dozen other bird species now breed and visiting birds have unintentionally brought other organisms along too. The island now has spiders, slugs and even earthworms.

## LOO BREAK

Not all great journeys cover miles and miles. In the rainforests of Central and South America, the most challenging adventure of a sloth's existence occurs about once a week, when it needs to answer nature's call. The rest of the time, the sloth hangs peacefully upside-down in one favourite tree by its huge, curved claws, eating leaves, sleeping and usually moving no faster than 4m a minute. However, when it's time for the weekly pee and poo, the sloth inches its way down from its tree and travels across the ground (at a positively breakneck 32m a minute) the short distance to its regular latrine or midden near the base of the tree, where it does the necessary and buries the evidence before returning to the branches. It's been suggested that, by using the same loo spot every time, the sloth is providing its favourite tree with a regular supply of nourishing manure.

## MESSAGE FROM AFRICA

One of the biggest leaps in understanding of bird migration happened in the spring of 1822, when a White Stork (*Ciconia ciconia*) arrived near Mecklenburg in Germany. The locals were familiar enough with the species – dozens of them showed up each spring to nest on the rooftops, departing to grounds unknown with their grown-up babies in autumn. This particular stork, however, carried a very obvious clue as to where it had been – a large arrow piercing its neck. The stork was shot and the arrow analysed; it proved to be of Central African origin. This discovery sounded the death knell for the prevailing theories of the time – that summer-visiting birds spent their winters asleep in lakes or that they flew to the moon.

Go anywhere nice on your holidays?

## HIGHEST BIRD FLIER

*A flock of migrating Bar-headed Geese (Anser indicus) were seen in the Himalayas travelling at 8,839m high. These geese habitually migrate at extreme altitudes and have modified blood chemistry to help them extract more oxygen from that rarefied mountain air.*

## THE SECRETIVE EEL

Even very familiar animals may have their secrets from us. One enduring mystery is where the European Eel (*Anguilla anguilla*) goes to spawn. We still don't know for sure but the likeliest spot is the Sargasso Sea in the North Atlantic, as here is where the very youngest eels have been observed. These babies are see-through, leaf-shaped and rather pathetic creatures, which do not feed but instead wait for ocean currents to bring them inshore. From there they start to grow into eel-shaped animals and head inland. Unlike salmon they don't have to stick to waterways to do this but may swarm across dry land or tunnel through damp sand. Finally they make it to a suitable river, pond or lake and stay there for some years, growing big and fat. Then they stop feeding and head back to the sea, to spawn and die.

## A PLAGUE OF CANNIBALISTIC LOCUSTS

The Desert Locust (*Schistocerca gregaria*) is a nightmare animal across parts of Africa, Asia and the Middle East, capable of doing untold damage to crops when it undertakes one of its devastating mass migrations. Swarms can cover 200km a day and will eat practically any plant material in their path; they can cross sea and desert, and only mountain ranges and rainforest will deter them. Recent research suggests that the swarms, which occur when breeding conditions are ideal, are triggered to set off on their journeys when a shortage of food (caused by too many locusts in one place) leads to some locusts turning on each other with thoughts of lunch. The efforts of the majority to escape the aggressors sets in motion the great plague.

Would you like to join our swarm?

No thanks, I already belong to a plague.

## ONE BIG PUSH

The bird that does perform the longest non-stop flight is a long-billed, rather handsome wader called the Bar-tailed Godwit (*Limosa lapponica*). One subspecies of this bird (*L. l. bauri*) nests in Alaska and winters in New Zealand, and once breeding is over the godwit population makes the trip from A to Z in a single, epic flight of some 10,000km, taking about eight days to do it. They do all this without the benefit of an in-flight movie and duty-free perfume, and the crossing is far out over the Pacific, meaning that these essentially non-swimming birds don't even give themselves the option of a rest on the way; it's thought that the risk of predation by taking a coastal route must be greater than the risk of dying from exhaustion or dehydration on the over-sea option.

Personal log.
Day five.
More sea.
Bored now.

## JUST KEEP SWIMMING

The great sea turtles are well known for being epic travellers. With the advent of satellite tracking technology, we are starting to find out just how epic – a tagged female Leatherback Turtle (*Dermochelys coriacea*) was tracked by satellite for 647 days before her transmitter failed, in which time she covered at least 20,557km and went from Indonesia to Oregon and many places in between. Given that Leatherbacks can also dive to depths of 1,200m, her actual journey could have been even longer.

### LONGEST INSECT FLIGHT

The appropriately named Globe Skimmer dragonfly (Pantala flavescens), which occurs across almost the entire southern hemisphere, may be the furthest flier among insects, with evidence that it habitually crosses the Arabian Sea from India to southern Africa (about 8,000km).

## COMING DOWN THE MOUNTAIN

Migrating from cold to warm places doesn't have to mean a dramatic change in latitude – it could also be simply a change of altitude. Many animals that breed on high mountains come down the slopes for a warmer winter. In the UK, three bird species that breed on the very highest mountain tops all have different strategies for when winter comes. The Dotterel (*Charadrius morinellus*) leaves the country altogether, wintering in north Africa or the Middle East. Most Snow Buntings (*Plectrophenax nivalis*) leave the mountains and many flock to the warmer coasts, where food is easier to find. However, the hardy Ptarmigan (*Lagopus mutus*) just moves a relatively short distance down the mountain slopes to spend winter at a slightly lower altitude.

## RED TIDE

Christmas Island, in the Indian Ocean, covers only 135km² but is home to some 120 million Christmas Island Red Crabs (*Gecarcoidea natalis*), one of 13 species of land crabs that live on the island. The crabs aren't that obvious all the time as they live in burrows, but when it's time for them to mate and lay their eggs in the sea, they take over the whole island as they travel to the coast, turning roads red as they swarm along. Road closures and diversions, plus purpose-built 'crab crossings' help protect them from being squashed by vehicles on their 18-day outward and return journey. Luckily for the island's human inhabitants, the massive disruption this causes only happens about twice a decade.

Maybe we should try this again next month...

## LONGEST LAND ANIMAL MIGRATION

The longest walk (discounting those of certain intrepid humans doing it for charity) is undertaken by Reindeer (*Rangifer tarandus*). North American herds (where they are known as Caribou) following the Porcupine River travel up to 5,000km a year between their calving grounds and winter feeding areas.

# CHAPTER 5

# EXTREME EXPERIENCES

For a species which evolved on the African plains, we humans have done rather well at exploiting environments to which we are completely physically unsuited. Of course, we are particularly good at manipulating our environment and also we are able to make things to protect ourselves from all kinds of natural hazards. Take all that away though and the book of impressive human accomplishments would suddenly become a lot thinner – you wouldn't catch Sir Ranulph Fiennes running to the North Pole in his birthday suit, for example. While few animals can rival us for versatility, some of them can do specific things which we couldn't even dream of and probably would never want to anyway. This chapter is about extreme adventures in the animal world – animals which survive in the most inhospitable places or have other lifestyle adaptations which place them far outside the 'norm'.

## HIGHEST JUMPER

*Froghoppers (superfamily Cercopoidea) are bouncers par excellence, able to jump 70cm vertically, meaning these little insects outperform the fleas.*

## LEAVE IT TO DADDY

One of the most famous of all animal extremists is the Emperor Penguin (*Aptenodytes forsteri*), able to endure the Antarctic winter out on the pack ice and, even more impressively, spending those long, chilly weeks nurturing the next generation. The female Emperors sensibly head off to the sea before winter sets in, each first laying an egg, which her mate transfers carefully (and quickly) to his feet. He folds his paunch over the egg and then shuffles up close to the other males and prepares for a long, boring and uncomfortable two months of standing almost motionless while being battered by some of the fiercest wind-chill imaginable. When the egg finally hatches the tiny new chick survives on a glandular secretion produced by the long-suffering father, before mum returns from the seas with a bellyful of fish.

## INVISIBLE GIANTS

The discovery of a new species is always exciting, and sometimes surprising, especially when that new species is a large mammal, which you would have thought someone would have noticed before. In 1992 a 90kg antelope-like animal was found in Vietnam, living in dense mountainous forests miles from human settlements. The Saola (*Pseudoryx nghetinhensis*) has been placed in a brand new genus due to a variety of unique anatomical features, including long, back-curved horns. The Saola is not the only large mammal to elude the scientists. Another is the very rare Bornean Rhino (*Dicerorhinus sumatrensis harrissoni*), which was not photographed in the wild until 2006 (and then by a motion-sensitive remote camera trap – better at standing still for ages than even the most patient photographer, and less smelly).

### DEEPEST DIVER (BIRDS)

*The Emperor Penguin (Aptenodytes forsteri) has reached depths of 565m, well beyond any other bird. The flying bird that dives deepest is Brünnich's Guillemot (Uria lomvia), which looks very much like a penguin but is an auk and can fly (just about) on its short, flipper-like wings. It can dive to 210m.*

## SALT AND AMMONIA

The mineral-rich and thermal spring-filled waters of Lake Natron in Africa's Rift Valley make it hostile to most animal life; it has a pH of more than 10, making it almost as alkaline as ammonia. Evaporation in the dry season concentrates the salt level even further. The few organisms that thrive in the shallow salty water out in the middle of the lake include billions of cyanobacteria (also known as blue-green algae). These are the staple diet of the Lesser Flamingos (*Phoenicopterus minor*) which nest on the lake during the dry season. These birds have tough skin on their feet and legs to resist the caustic – and hot – water.

## LATE BLOOMERS

Most insects spend the bulk of their lifespan in an immature form, devoted to eating and growing before a brief, glorious adulthood of frantic sex. One of the most extreme examples of this comes from the cicadas (family Cicadidae) – large-winged insects famous for making an incessant chirping racket on sultry summer evenings. Some cicada species are among the most long-lived of insects, spending 17 years living underground in their immature form. When they finally reach full maturity, they climb out and up a tree, and the adult insects emerge from the bodies of the nymphs, each leaving a paper-thin shell of nymphal casing still clinging by its empty legs to the tree trunk. The adults live for five weeks at the most; no wonder they make as much noise about it as they can.

*Just 15 more years and I can go outside...*

## THE DIVING BELL AND THE SPIDER

If you are an air-breathing animal that wants to live underwater, either you'll need to surface to breathe every so often or you'll need to bring a supply of air underwater with you. The Water Spider (*Argyroneta aquatica*) has taken option two and can be credited with the invention of the diving bell. The female builds a large underwater ball of silk. She then stocks it with air, which she collects from the surface in the form of air bubbles trapped in the hairs on her abdomen. The diving bell provides her with a refuge in which she eats her prey, mates, lays eggs and moults her skin. Males build smaller and simpler bells, and spend more of their time out in the open water, using air trapped on their bodies as a portable breathing supply.

---

### MOST RESTRICTED RANGE OF ANY VERTEBRATE

*The Devil's Hole Pupfish (Cyprinodon diabolis) lives in a 20m by 3m, spring-fed pool in the middle of a desert in Nevada and occurs naturally nowhere else. The few hundred fish in the pool don't even use all of it but stick to the end where the algae they eat grows.*

---

## SEABIRD SECRETS OF ETERNAL YOUTH

On the subject of long-lived seabirds, there exists a photograph showing the zoologist George Dunnet with a newly ringed Fulmar (*Fulmarus glacialis*), another kind of petrel, in 1952. Nothing remarkable about that, but there are also photos showing Professor Dunnet with the very same Fulmar in 1982, when it was recaptured and its ring checked, and again in 1992. No prizes for guessing which of them is showing its age more. Why do seabirds live so long? One reason is that they are slow to mature and slow to reproduce, having only one or two chicks a year. Another is that they generally face few threats in their adult lives, but their breeding success is very much at the mercy of variable feeding conditions. Long life helps the population to endure prolonged spells of poor feeding conditions and consequent reproductive failure.

## BEARS IN SPACE

Not actual bears. That would never work. But studies have recently shown that tiny animals called tardigrades (phylum Tardigrada), aka 'water bears', can survive in open space for at least ten days, enduring solar winds and a complete vacuum. These cute microscopic, eight-legged animals are among the toughest of all creatures. Studies have shown that they can live through temperatures ranging from -273°C to 151°C, can cope with 1,000 times the radiation it would take to kill a human and can be revived after being totally dried out for ten years. The name for creatures like this which can cope with various different extreme conditions is 'polyextremophiles' – try to use it in a conversation today.

*Engage!*

## SAFE SLEEP

Wild animals don't have the luxury of a locked door and comfy bed, so for them sleep is risky, especially if they don't have a cosy nest or den. Many catch short bursts of sleep and their total sleep requirements are often far less than ours. One of the least sleepy of all animals is the Giraffe (*Giraffa camelopardalis*), which can get by on less than four hours in a 24-hour period. If you've seen how arduous it is for a Giraffe to lower itself down to take a drink, you'll understand why it doesn't easily curl up on the savannah for a nap – it will often sleep standing up. Giraffes are also sometimes observed sleeping in a most peculiar contorted sitting posture, with the neck arching round so the head is resting on the ground or the hind legs. Obviously, getting up quickly from a posture like this in an emergency is going to be difficult but a bit easier than if they allowed themselves the luxury of sprawling out full length on the ground.

### LONGEST-LIVED MAMMAL

*In May 2007 a Bowhead Whale (Balaena mysticetus) with a harpoon embedded in its body was caught. The harpoon was of a kind that hadn't been made since the 1880s, suggesting that the whale was at least 130 years old.*

## FROG OF THE NORTH

Because of their inability to generate their own body heat, amphibians and reptiles tend not to occur in very cold places, leaving those to the warm-blooded birds and mammals. The amphibian that has evolved to cope best with chilliness is the Wood Frog (*Rana sylvatica*) of North America, which can be found inside the Arctic Circle. So how does it avoid freezing when it hibernates in winter? It doesn't. Its blood and some other body tissues can freeze solid – up to 65 per cent of the fluid in its body can freeze without killing the frog. Its biochemistry is adapted to minimize freezing and to prevent cell damage when freezing does occur.

## LIVE LONG AND PROSPER

It's been said that one reason hamsters are popular family pets is because they help children learn all about death. Like other small mammals, they have woefully short lifespans and rarely last three years. But small doesn't always mean short-lived. Small birds can and do live much longer than similarly sized mammals. Recoveries of ringed wild birds have shown that most of our familiar small garden birds can make it well into double figures (although, of course, predation means that few do). Small seabirds live even longer. One Storm Petrel (*Hydrobates pelagicus*), a sparrow-sized seabird, was ringed as an adult in 1962 then recaptured alive and well in 1994, making it at least 33 years old.

## DEEPEST-SWIMMING FISH

*So far, the fish found deepest in the sea is Abyssobrotula galatheae, in the Puerto Rican Trench at 8,372m. Studying such deep-sea fish is extremely difficult, as they are adapted to live in the high pressures of such deep water and can't survive closer to the surface.*

## SLUG-HOPPER

It's not often you get the opportunity to describe a slug accurately as 'bouncy' or 'vivacious'. Most of the time, the Dromedary Jumping Slug (*Hemphillia dromedarius*) of Canada just slimes slowly along like any other slug. However, if it is attacked by any of its numerous predators, it starts thrashing about like a maniac, using its large 'hump' to push itself up and over in a repeated manoeuvre, which, although not exactly 'jumping', is probably as close to it as you're ever going to get from a slug.

## DRINK IN THE DESERT

Water conservation is key for desert animals and some also have clever tricks for getting a drink in unpromising arid environments. In Namibia, a shiny black beetle called *Selevinia betpakdalaensis* lives in the dunes, not that far from the sea. When the wind blows an early-morning fog in from the sea, the beetle assumes a curious posture, with head down, bottom up and legs spread out. Water from the fog condenses on the various ridges on its carapace, and as droplets are formed they roll downhill via the waxy, hydrophobic troughs in the carapace towards the beetle's head, enabling it to take a drink. The locals have emulated this trick of the so-called 'fog-basking beetle' and make similarly designed 'fog-catchers' to obtain water for themselves.

## THE HEAT IS ON

The Giant Tube Worm (*Riftia pachyptila*) is a formidable beast. For a start, it is massive, growing to 2.5m long. Even more impressively, it lives in what must be one of the most inhospitable habitat types on Earth – miles deep in the Pacific Ocean, in close proximity to the fierce sulphurous heat of hydrothermal vents. It lives inside a protective tube of hard minerals, from which protrudes a red fluffy 'plume' that takes in hydrogen sulphite and other dissolved chemicals in the water. It has no digestive system at all; instead all of its dietary needs are met by a population of bacteria that lives inside its body and turns the stuff absorbed by the plume into useable nutrients.

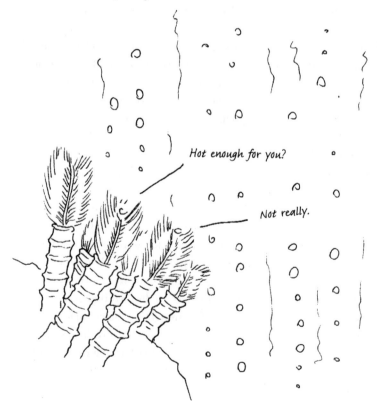

Hot enough for you?

Not really.

## ONE WAY TO SKIN A DORMOUSE

You might think that having no fur at all would be a good plan for a desert mammal. That might help keep things cool in the heat of the day but desert nights can be very cold, and bare skin also loses too much water in arid conditions. A better bet is a very well-insulating fur coat that helps maintain an even body temperature for the animal that's wearing it. The Desert Dormouse (*Selevinia betpakdalaensis*) lives in the central Asian deserts and is unusual among mammals in moulting not just its fur but its actual skin. As patches of old fur-covered skin come off, they reveal new skin that's already covered with fully grown fur, meaning the dormouse is never without a full coat of insulating fluff.

### ANIMAL LIVING AT THE HIGHEST ALTITUDE

The Alpine Chough (*Pyrrhocorax graculus*), a shiny black, yellow-billed crow, lives high in mountainous areas and has been seen at 8,235m (the summit of Everest is 8,848m). The highest-living mammal is the Large-eared Pika (*Ochtona macrotis*) of Asia. This stocky rabbit-like creature is found at up to 6,130m.

## THREE-DAY WONDER

The other lifespan extreme is provided by the phylum Gastrotricha. If you know your Latin you'll know that 'gastrotrich' means 'stomach hair', and these creatures are little more than tiny (the biggest reach just 3mm) hair-shaped swimming stomachs. From birth to death they live for just three days, but then again many gastrotrichs reproduce by cloning themselves (parthenogenesis), so in another sense it could be said that they live forever.

## FASTEST BIRD

*In the air, the fastest-moving bird is the Peregrine Falcon (Falco peregrinus), which can hit 322km an hour in a steep dive, while in level flight the White-throated Needletail (Hirundapus caudacutus), an Asian species of swift, has been clocked at 170km an hour. Ostriches (Struthio camelus) run faster than any other bird, at 72km an hour.*

## CLAM OF AGES (AND AGES)

It's been suggested that the more boring your life is, the longer you'll live. Lifestyles don't get much more routine than that of a filter-feeding bivalve mollusc, and it is one of these that is the oldest animal on record. The clam in question, an Ocean Quahog (*Arctica islandica*), was dredged up along with many others from deep waters off Iceland and analysis of the growth patterns of its shells revealed that it had lived there for 405 years.

No, trust me, nothing EVER happens here.

## PLAYING CHICKEN FOR FISH

Remember those flamingos in Lake Natron? There is another animal leading an even more risky lifestyle in those hot and salty waters – the cichlid fish *Oreochromis alcalicus*. It lives around the hot spring inlets of this lake and others in the Rift Valley, feeding on the abundant algae that grow there. Its forays down to the richest algal supplies are fraught with danger though, as the water here is hot enough to kill. So the fish makes swift, dashing visits, grabbing a mouthful at a time. Should one linger too long, it will, effectively, poach itself and thus not pass on its too-reckless genes to the next generation.

## HAVE A NICE DAY

Mayflies (order Emphemeroptera) famously live for just one day. Of course, that's just their adult lives. Prior to this they lived many months as aquatic nymphs, munching algae on river beds. Once they do mature, they completely lose the ability to feed; the adult mouthparts are essentially non-existent and the once-busy digestive tract is now full of nothing but air. Now the few remaining hours of their lives are devoted to the pursuit of the opposite sex, in a rush to reproduce before they run out of energy and die. To further this goal, mayflies make up for their lack of feeding equipment by a surfeit of breeding equipment – males have two penises and the females two corresponding receptacles.

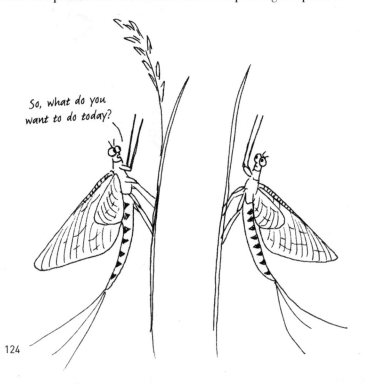

## DEEPEST DIVER (MAMMALS)

*Among mammals, Sperm Whales (Physeter macrocephalus) are capable of diving deeper than any other, occasionally reaching up to 3,000m, though some beaked whales (family Ziphiidae) average longer and deeper dives overall. The deepest-diving seal is the Southern Elephant Seal (Microunga leonina), with one tagged animal diving down to 2,388m.*

## SAVING WATER

All animals need water for their cells to function properly. Animals adapted for a life in very arid conditions need to hang on to every molecule of water they can and have come up with some interesting ways of doing this. Kangaroo rats (genus *Dipodomys*) have perhaps the most efficient kidneys around, capable of recycling some 90 per cent of the water they need – that's four times more efficient than the human kidney – and results in urine five times more concentrated than ours. The rest of their water requirement comes from their diet; they can metabolize water from the hydrogen in their food plus the oxygen they breathe.

## HEARTSTOPPING

Hummingbirds' fantastically high metabolism demands a very rapid heart rate, often well over 1,000 beats a minute when the bird is in full hover mode. That tiny heart is capable of winding right down to a positively lethargic 50 beats a minute at night though, to preserve precious energy. Sleeping hummingbirds enter a hibernation-like state called torpor, whereby all bodily functions slow down to a crawl and the body temperature plummets. Obviously they are easy prey if any predator should find them in this insensible state but the energetic demands of an alert hummer mean it could not last through the night without feeding.

## SPECIALLY SPECIALIZED

Many species of fish that live in dark cave pools have evolved to become blind, rerouting the energy that would be consumed by a visual system to other, more useful functions. One is the Alabama Cavefish (*Speoplatyrhinus poulsoni*), which is not only blind but has no eyes at all. It has only ever been found in the subterranean pools of Key Cave National Wildlife Reserve in Alabama, even though these pools are part of a much larger network of underground waterways; it seems to have exceptionally poor powers of dispersal. A survey of some 120 other local pools failed to produce any more records of Alabama Cavefish and the species is classed as endangered. The 100 or so that do exist survive in an ecosystem fuelled by the droppings of the Gray Bats (*Myotis grisescens*) that breed in the non-waterlogged parts of the caves.

---

## LONGEST MAMMAL HIBERNATION

*Controlled experiments showed that the Eastern Pygmy-possum (Cercartetus nanus) could sleep for more than a year, living off its stored body fat. In natural conditions, Colombian Ground Squirrels (Citellus columbianus) have been observed to hibernate for up to 238 days.*

---

## I LIKE IT HERE

While some animals travel the world every year of their lives, others are remarkable for their tendency not to go anywhere, and not always because their bodies aren't built to move. The Eurasian Treecreeper (*Certhia familiaris*) rarely strays beyond 20km of where it was born, despite being perfectly able to fly. The Tawny Owl (*Strix aluco*) is almost as sedentary. One of the least adventurous insects is the Frigate Island Beetle (*Polposipus herculeanus*), with a record lifetime movement of 19m. It is flightless, but at 3cm long with six very sturdy walking legs you'd expect it to be capable of a bit more than that, especially as it can live in its adult form for seven years or more.

## WATER-WALKERS

There are several ways to not sink when you enter the water. You can float (birds are good at this, being lightweight with water-repelling oils on their plumage). You can balance on the water's surface tension (only works for very small, very light animals with wide-spreading legs, like pond-skater insects). You can swim (many animals can do this, some better than others). Or, if you are a basilisk lizard (genus *Basiliscus*), you can just run like hell. Basilisks are quite small lizards but would undoubtedly sink if dropped into a lake from a great height. However, they can also run extremely fast on their hind legs and this enables them to cross up to 20m of water before they start to sink. Their broad feet help keep them upright, while the long tail aids their balance. This clever trick, a way to escape predators, has earned them the nickname 'Jesus Christ lizards'.

### FASTEST SWIMMERS

The two species of sailfish (genus Istiophorus) are the fastest things in the water, swimming at 110km an hour. The quickest mammalian swimmer is the Killer Whale (Orcinus orca), at 65km an hour, while Gentoo Penguins (Pygoscelis papua) win for the birds, swimming at about 36km an hour.

## CHAPTER 6

# PECULIAR PASSIONS

What would you do for love? History documents plenty of heroic – and horrific – human actions intended to further the cause of a lover trying to win over the girl or boy of their dreams. Deciding on and then successfully courting the right partner for you is a major challenge in human existence and different cultures have a wide array of methods to help make the process easier. The same is true in the animal world, where virtually all couplings happen with the objective of successful parenting. Some animals are simply looking for as many quick flings as possible and have no role in the care of their own young. Others form lifelong bonds and so are seeking a partner who will consistently deliver good childcare over an extended period as well as good genetic material to make healthy offspring in the first place. Here we look at some of the strategies animals use to make sweet, sweet love.

## POLYGYNANDRY

You know you've got an interesting sex life when animal biologists have to invent a new word to describe it. Polygynandry is a combination of polygyny (when one male pairs with several females) and polyandry (when one female pairs with several males) and describes the breeding system of a rather dull-looking small European songbird called the Dunnock (*Prunella modularis*). Depending on the balance of the sexes, female Dunnocks regularly pair up with two males. One (the 'alpha') is favoured over the other (the 'beta') and gets more mating opportunities; but both males form a bond with the female that lasts the season and both help her rear her brood; however, those males may themselves also be 'time-shared' with other females. Polygynandry has also been observed in some other birds and accurately describes the society of the Bonobo or Pygmy Chimpanzee (*Pan paniscus*).

## DEATH BY SEX

Dying immediately after breeding is commonplace in many animal groups but not among mammals. One exception is provided by the antechinuses (genus *Antechinus*), small, pointy-nosed marsupials from Australia and New Guinea. Both sexes only breed once in their short lifetimes, so mating takes on great importance, especially for the males, who put everything they've got into a copulatory frenzy lasting through August and September. Each male stays close to every receptive female he finds for a 12-hour period, mating repeatedly and guarding her from other males' advances. This guarding rarely succeeds completely – most antechinus litters are of multiple paternity – so it's on to the next female to repeat the process. At the end of the mating season, the exhausted males die, and the only slightly less exhausted females follow a few months later, as soon as their litter is weaned.

*He said he felt all shagged out, and then...*

## BACHELOR PAD

Fish can do many wonderful things but you wouldn't necessarily think that heavy construction work would be one of them. Just to prove you wrong, the male Three-spined Stickleback (*Gasterosteus aculeatus*) is a nest-builder extraordinaire. He makes a tubular nest out of water weeds, sticking it together with his own kidney secretions and anchoring it in place with pebbles. Once the nest is complete, he displays in front of it, exhibiting his eye-catching scarlet belly to any passing females. If she likes the look of the nest, a female will come inside and lay eggs there, whereupon the male boots her out and fertilizes the eggs. For the next week or so he guards the nest while the eggs develop safely inside.

## KISS, MARRY, THROW OFF A CLIFF

Kittiwakes (*Rissa tridactyla*) are elegant gulls which, unlike many other gull species, have a very close tie to the sea. They nest in large colonies on cliff faces, often choosing precariously narrow ledges on which to build their seaweed nests. It is necessary, therefore, for both young and adult Kittiwakes to be good at not falling off cliffs. An incubating adult could take its egg with it if it gets blown from its nest, while a youngster that can't yet fly has an even more pressing need not to fall down. So courting Kittiwakes indulge in playful wrestling on the cliff face, each trying to heft the other off the edge. Those that best pass this test of innate not-falling-off skill will be the most desirable partners, likely to parent equally sure-footed babies and take good care of them too.

## MONKEY BUSINESS

Many people will insist that humans are not meant for monogamy, arguing that most other mammals are either polygamous or promiscuous in their habits. While that's quite true, it should be noted that among our own order of mammals, the primates, monogamy is commoner than it is among most other groups. In one monkey species, the Saddle-back Tamarin (*Saguinus fuscicollis*) of South America, monogamy, polyandry or polygyny may all be practised at different times. The most common arrangement is one female pairing up with two males. She always has twins, and when they are born she hands one over to each boyfriend (though only one of the two males can be the father) and doesn't take them back, except when she needs to feed them.

Here, take these. I'm going foraging with the girls now.

## MR BOOMBASTIC

Many endangered animals in the world do themselves no favours by adhering to very definite and elaborate courtship behaviour. Take the Kakapo, a corpulent and flightless green parrot from New Zealand. When it's time to mate (which only happens in years when the local rimu trees produce a heavy crop) the males walk up to 7km uphill to the lekking grounds, where they make bowl-shaped depressions in the ground and stand in them, making resonant booming sounds (the farthest-carrying bird sounds in the world) to attract females (which also have to walk long distances to reach them). Given the extreme rarity of the species, a male may boom fruitlessly every night for months, losing much of his cherished body fat in the process. The species' reproductive rate is, fairly obviously, very slow, and although conservation efforts are paying off, its recovery from near extinction will take many years.

### A HOLE NEW EXPERIENCE

Look away now (if you haven't already), readers of a more sensitive disposition. The private life of the Boto or Amazonian River Dolphin (*Inia geoffrensis*) includes something that even humans don't indulge in – nasal sex. These freshwater dolphins, which have long beaks and shocking pink skin are among the many species of animals that have been observed engaging in homosexual activities, and one such activity involves male A penetrating the blowhole of male B. As the blowhole, which is analogous to the human nostrils, is located on top of the head, the two dolphins can achieve this unusual form of congress while maintaining a natural right-way-up swimming position.

### STUCK ON YOU

Deep-sea anglerfish (family Ceratiidae) are thinly distributed in their habitat and they have formed an unusual solution to the consequent problem of infrequent mating opportunities. The male, a fraction the size of the female, is more or less unable to feed on his own and so seeks out a female, detecting her by scent. Once he finds one he bites into her underside and releases an enzyme which starts to digest both his mouth lining and her skin, so the two fish become fused, their blood vessels connected. The male's body thus derives its nutrients directly from the female's. Over a long period the male's body slowly breaks down and wastes away, leaving just his testes, which release their sperm when the female's body sends a chemical signal that she's about to release her eggs.

## MUCK-SPREADING

It takes all sorts, and female Hippopotamuses (*Hippopotamus amphibius*) have very specific – and very odd – ideas about what impresses them in a mate. A dominant male Hippo attracts a harem of females and he both keeps them in line and shows off his strength to his rivals by performing a lovely ritual called 'dung-showering'. This involves simultaneously urinating, defecating and spinning the tail like a propeller, resulting in a smelly shower for anyone, Hippo or otherwise, who is foolish enough to be standing nearby.

## DOWN THE GARDEN PATH

Red velvet mites (family Trombidiidae) are tiny soil animals, related to spiders, which are bright red and look fuzzy under a microscope. Males have an unusual courtship tactic – they lay down twirling trails of silk through the earth and leaf litter to attract females. Following the trail, the female then finds parcels of the male's sperm, deposited in prominent spots like little decorations. If she's sufficiently impressed, she'll sit on the sperm. If another male finds this 'garden of love' though, he will destroy it and replace it with one of his own.

## MY BEAUTIFUL BALLOON

Male birds are often more colourful than females, and in those species where the males are particularly colourfully and elaborately plumed, there is often a spectacular display used to show off the feathers to their best advantage. In the case of the frigatebirds (family Fregatidae), strong-flying seabirds which can't afford to compromise their aerial abilities with fancy feathers, the display involves the inflation of a patch of colourful throat skin (or 'gular pouch' if you want the technical term). Males gather in trees and blow up their pouches to massive proportions, creating a great scarlet balloon much bigger than their heads and wider than the rest of their bodies. They then waggle their balloons enticingly at passing females.

## GOLDEN SHOWER

Male Old World porcupines (family Hystricidae) win over potential mates by standing on their hind legs and generously spraying the lucky female with urine. If the female decides she likes this treatment, she will in due course crouch down, flatten her quills and allow him to gingerly mount her. If the male or his wee does not meet her quality standards, she will attack him with tremendous ferocity and drive him away. The traumatic courtship process happens only once a year, which might be considered a blessing for both sexes.

## YOUR ARM IN MARRIAGE

Squids and octopuses (class Cephalopoda) come in two sexes, rather than being hermaphrodite like many other molluscs. One of the special characteristics of most male cephalopods is his 'mating arm' or hectocotylus, which is used to transfer his sperm from his penis to the female's body. In the case of the group of octopuses called argonauts or paper nautiluses (genus *Argonauta*), the hectocolytus breaks off during mating and stays stuck in the female's body, wriggling about as if still alive. This led scientists to initially classify it as some kind of bizarre parasitic worm.

## WORST LOVE-CHEAT

*Many happily paired-up birds will seize any opportunity for some sneaky extra-marital sex. A recent study showed that a gob-smacking 95 per cent of female Saltmarsh Sparrows (Ammodramus caudacutus) cheated on their mates each nesting season.*

## SWINGING BOTH WAYS

Hermaphrodites have more fun, as the saying goes (or should go). Quite a few of our familiar animals have both male and female parts, including the humble Garden Snail (*Helix aspersa*), and for them sex is a protracted and confusing affair. When two snails meet and decide (after a lengthy spell of mutual exploration) that they like each other, each thrusts a 'love dart' into the other. These tiny, calcium-based weapons apparently prepare each snail's female parts for copulation. Then the two penetrate each other and copulation is completed. If a snail's penis shears off during copulation (an alarmingly frequent complication), it can continue to mate with other snails using just its female parts.

## ULTIMATE FREELOADER

If you're a male whose idea of a good life is sponging off a willing female forever, read on, for the Green Spoonworm (*Bonellia viridis*) has got this one licked. Males don't simply live off the female, they live in her, dwelling within her genital sac and providing sperm as required, while she provides all the nutrients they need. Green Spoonworms even get a choice (sort of) as to which sex they will be. Larvae that land on the sea floor mature into females, but larvae that come into contact with an adult female are masculinized by a substance called bonellin, which is produced by her skin.

## TWO-TIMING

Whalers named the right whales (genus *Eubalaena*) as they did because they were the 'right' ones to go after, being easy to find and kill. They are also the 'right' whales if you are looking for a whale with, well, massive testes. They are not the largest of the whales but there are no more impressive family jewels on earth than these 500kg (each) whoppers and they are also big relative to body size. Big balls is a sure sign of a species in which intense competition between males takes place and promiscuity is rife, and proof of this was provided when scientists observed a female Northern Right Whale (*Eubalaena glacialis*) copulating with two males simultaneously.

### GAYEST ANIMAL

The Roseate Cockatoo or Galah (Eolophus roseicapilla), native to Australia, forms same-sex pairs 44 per cent of the time in captivity.

## BY FORCE

Those friendly quacking Mallards (*Anas platyrhynchos*) on your local park pond have a dark secret. Ducks and geese are among the few birds that possess penises, and males sometimes use their very large, spiral-shaped organs to devastating advantage, forcing themselves upon unwilling females in violent 'gang rapes'. The females do have a trick up their sleeve as well, though. Their vaginas have numerous extra outpouchings, which are 'dead ends'. Some of these may grow in spirals that twist in the opposite direction to the male's penis. So while the females may not be able to protect themselves from unwanted advances, they can help ensure that the male attacker does not get to pass on his genes.

## FREE LOVE

Remember the Bonobos, polygynandrous apes? These rather dainty creatures have a very different way of life from their close relative, the Common Chimpanzee (*Pan troglodytes*). While your Common Chimp is a highly strung animal, frequently indulging in acts of noisy aggression, for Bonobos it's all about sex. In a Bonobo group the only couplings that are not observed are between mother and son, anything else goes. They are the only animals besides ourselves to indulge regularly in oral and missionary-position sex, and same-sex contact is frequent (the male version charmingly nicknamed 'penis fencing'). Most interestingly, most of this sexual activity is nothing to do with reproduction but serves to build and maintain bonds within the group.

It's very nice to meet you too.

## BIG HUG

One of the UK's most charming road signs is the one depicting a toad, displayed on roads that numbers of Common Toads (*Bufo bufo*) cross on their way to their spawning ponds. Toads are slow walkers at the best of times, but on the way to spawn the female often has the additional encumbrance of a male on her back, hanging on firmly with both arms wrapped tightly around her. This position, called amplexus, is seen in all toads and in some species persists for an amazingly long time. One pair of the South American species *Atelopus oxyrhynchus* is on record for spending 125 days in amplexus on the long migration to the streams where they breed. Hard work for the female but tougher for the male, who becomes quite emaciated by the time the pair reaches their destination. At least he more or less guarantees that he will be the male who gets to fertilize her eggs.

## THAT'S GOT TO HURT

If you've ever been woken by the sound of domestic moggies making love outside, you'll know how loudly a female cat can scream. She does so for good reason. The male cat's penis is armed with backward-pointing spines, so when he withdraws he causes the female considerable pain (which stimulates ovulation). Male Lions (*Panthera leo*), like their smaller relatives, have similarly spiny bits and they will mate with a receptive female up to 40 times a day for several days. Perhaps that explains the difference between a scream and a roar.

## SPERM WARS

When a male damselfly (suborder Zygoptera) gets together with a female, one of the first things he does is use his penis to empty out her spermatheca (a receptacle where sperm is stored until her eggs are ready). He does this because damselflies mate with several different partners over a short period, so there's every chance any given female damselfly has already mated with another male. This is just one example of sperm competition, whereby males try to ensure theirs is the only sperm that gets to do any fertilizing. Another tactic, seen in various mammals and other species, is the use of a 'copulatory plug' of sticky material, which blocks the female's vagina to further penetration after copulation – a sort of *ex post facto* chastity device.

## CAN I OFFER YOU A DRINK?

The African Wild Ass (*Equus africanus*) is the probable ancestor of the domestic donkey and is now very rare in the wild. It survives in a few desert areas in north-eastern Africa and, unlike many desert animals, it needs to drink water regularly. Dominant male asses, well aware of the importance of access to water, establish their territories in close proximity to a water source, and their 'ownership' of this vital resource makes them almost irresistible to passing females. The territorial boundaries are marked out with large heaps of dung, which provide a visual marker in the featureless desert surroundings, even when their aroma has diminished.

### A STAB IN THE DARK

Male bedbugs (family Cimicidae) don't really go in for the hearts-and-flowers approach to seduction. They don't even waste any time trying to locate an appropriate orifice on the female's body but instead just punch a random hole in the female's abdomen with their 'hypodermic genitalia' and inject their sperm straight into her body cavity. The sperm then migrates to her ovaries. This practice is called traumatic insemination and is seen in several invertebrate species, although bedbugs are unusual in that they do it exclusively. The process is not only impolite but also potentially harmful, leaving the female with an open wound, though in bedbugs females have evolved physiological traits that help minimize the damage.

## MY TWO DADS

Homosexual behaviour among wild animals is quite common and well documented. One interesting example comes from Australia, home of the very beautiful Black Swan (*Cygnus atratus*). Many Black Swan families consist of two males, plus a brood of cygnets. What happened to the mother? It is quite common for two male Black Swans to pair up, and a female will seek out a male couple as they will often have secured a better territory than a lone male. She teams up with them for as long as it takes for her to mate and lay her eggs. Whether she wants anything more to do with them after that is academic, as they chase her away and assume sole custody of the clutch. As males are bigger and stronger than females, chicks reared by a male pair are more likely to survive than those of a heterosexual pair.

---

### LONGEST ANIMAL PAIR BOND

*Many animals are long-lived and pair for life. Some species of parrots (order Psittaciformes) can live for 70 years or more and, as they become sexually active aged five or six, a pair could potentially stay together for several decades. However, they're unlikely to beat the record 86-year human marriage.*

---

## LET'S PRETEND

Parthenogenesis is when female animals produce cloned female babies without any need for copulation with a male. For those who like the idea of a male-free society, it's the way to go. In the case of the Desert Grassland Whiptail lizard of America (*Cnemidophorus uniparens*), all reproduction is by parthenogenesis but the lizards still need to 'act out' a male–female copulation to stimulate the production of the cloned eggs. Two females pair up, and over a period of up to two weeks they will engage in bouts of 'pseudocopulation', taking it in turns to mount each other. Without this interaction, neither will lay eggs.

### SHOW-OFFS

The Swedish word 'lek', meaning 'play', is much used in animal biology, as it describes one of the most entertaining spectacles you'll ever see in the natural world. Many species indulge in lekking, with birds like the Black Grouse (*Tetrao tetrix*) and Ruff (*Philomachus pugnax*) perhaps best known for it in the UK. Males of these species, which are much bigger and more strikingly plumaged than females, gather in traditional 'arenas' and perform extravagant, energetic and noisy displays together to attract females. They also indulge in frequent dust-ups when one gets too close to another, allowing the females to assess their fighting skills as well as their physical condition. The 'best' males inevitably get all the girls, the rest will have to try again the next day, or next year.

### I'M A LADY!

When Common Garter Snakes (*Thamnophis sirtalis*) wake up in the first warm days of spring in North America, sex is the first thing on their minds. Males emerge from hibernation first and when they detect the pheromones of a stirring female they hurry to the scene, so each female often has ten or more eager suitors to contend with. Sometimes, though, it's a male that is releasing the sexy smells, tricking the other males into approaching him instead. With lots of other males trying to get close to him, the trickster warms up more quickly than the other males and therefore can move more quickly to the scene when a bona fide female appears.

## GETTING THE BLUES

Showing off to the ladies is widespread in the bird world and accounts for the many colourful plumages and displays seen among male birds of all kinds. The bowerbirds (family Ptilonorhynchidae) do things slightly differently – they create an eye-catching construction (a bower) to which the females are attracted. Interestingly, the more elaborate the bower is, the duller in appearance is its builder. The Satin Bowerbird (*Ptilonorhynchus violaceus*) has a penchant for the colour blue, and the glossy blackish male decorates his bower with any different blue things as he can find. Perhaps this colour is favoured because the dull, greenish-brown female's bright blue eyes are easily her best feature.

## LONGEST COURTSHIP

*This is difficult to define, as animals that pair for life continue
to reinforce their bond indefinitely with courtship behaviours.
Among non-pairing animals that 'root, shoot and leave', some
snails spend up to six hours seducing each other between
meeting and mating.*

## A PLATYPUS AND HIS SPURS

One of the handful of known venomous mammals on Earth is
that renowned weirdo, the Platypus (*Ornithorhynchus
anatinus*). However, while the others (mostly small insect-
hunters like shrews) use their venom to disable their prey, the
Platypus dispenses its toxins through a rather impractical outlet
for that purpose – via bony spurs on the ankles of its hind legs.
Moreover, only the male's spurs produce venom (and mostly
during the breeding season), the female's spurs are rudimentary
and lack venom glands. Therefore, it seems probable that
Platypus venom is used by males against other males, in
combat over mating rights; its effects are not lethal but a good
dose would certainly convince a rival to try his luck elsewhere.

## SONG OF SONGS

Male birds of many species compete with each other and attract
females with songs. Much birdsong is just as delightful to
human ears as it is to those of female birds, but one of the most
brilliant is that of the male Superb Lyrebird (*Menura
novaehollandiae*) of Australia. As well as having a huge
repertoire of sounds of his own, this large songbird has
unparalleled powers of mimicry and incorporates into his song
the sounds of other local birds, from kookaburras and
cockatoos to bellbirds and scrub-wrens. He doesn't stop at

imitating other bird sounds either – depending on his location he might include car alarms, chainsaws, music from radios and even the sounds made by film crews as they record the performance for natural history TV programmes. The song is accompanied by a dramatic display of his long and beautiful tail feathers.

### COMPROMISING POSITION

If you're a Stump-tailed Macaque (*Macaca arctoides*), you'd be well advised to make sure you and your partner are alone before having a bit of nooky. These monkeys have a bad habit of launching ferocious attacks on other members of their troupe when the latter are at their most vulnerable – during orgasm. The victims of these sneaky attacks are almost always the dominant males, while the perpetrators tend to be either young males or females of any age. Researchers studying the behaviour have ruled out several possible motivations for the attacks and have concluded that the likeliest explanation is revenge – subordinate monkeys seizing their chance to punish the 'boss' for previous bullying behaviour.

### GIVE US A P

Ever pointed out a cute monkey in a zoo to a child, then had to quickly distract them when said monkey began doing something rather less than cute? Animals don't share our ideas about what's adorable and some of the sweetest-looking critters have some of the most unfortunate habits. Take the Northern Greater or Garnett's Galago (*Otolemur garnettii*), which

Damn! Why does it always rain when I ovulate?

you'll recognize as a kind of bushbaby – a charming, bug-eyed, bat-eared and fluffy-tailed little primate from Africa. This sweet fuzzball has a behaviour that biologists call 'urine-washing', whereby it carefully pees into its cupped hand, then applies the urine to both hands and both feet. Wherever it goes after this, it leaves a trace of its own unique pee-smell behind, to inform other galagos of its territorial boundaries. In a surprising twist, a male galago will also pee directly on to any ovulating females in his social circle – perhaps this is the bushbaby equivalent of a love bite.

## ORGY ON THE SEA-BED

In common with many other molluscs, the Spotted Sea Hare (*Aplysia dactylomela*), a very widespread sea slug, is a hermaphrodite, so any other Spotted Sea Hare it encounters is a potential sexual partner. If there are lots of them around and all are in the mood for some action, it is not unusual for it to form 'mating chains' consisting of several animals, all linked together with the animal at one end performing a male role only, the one at the other a female role only and those in between performing both roles simultaneously. Another interesting thing about sea hares is that their egg strings look just like spaghetti.

## THE OLDEST PROFESSION

Most birds are monogamous… on paper. Given the opportunity, though, few will resist the opportunity of a brief, no-strings liaison with a neighbour – both sexes benefit from a bit of extra genetic mingling. In the case of the Adélie Penguin (*Pygoscelis adeliae*) there is an extra factor involved. These birds construct nests of pebbles to help keep their eggs clear of the cold Antarctic ground; male courtship involves offering pebbles to a prospective mate. Pebbles are hard to find and pebble thefts commonplace in the close-knit colonies, although the thieves receive harsh physical punishment if caught. Female Adélies, however, avoid punishment by exchanging pebbles for sex. One female was observed to obtain 62 extra pebbles for her and her partner's nest by soliciting them from nearby unpaired males.

So... what do I get for TWO pebbles?

## BIG WOMEN

Sexual dimorphism describes animals in which the sexes look distinctly different. More often than not, males are bigger, but in birds of prey it's the other way round. The Sparrowhawk (*Accipiter nisus*), a bird-hunter, shows the most sexual dimorphism of any UK bird of prey, with females sometimes twice as heavy as males. This means males can do the hunting and females the nest-guarding while the chicks are small, with the females joining in with hunting when the growing chicks need larger lunches. It also enables the pair to exploit a much wider range of potential prey species between them than they

could if they were the same size. However, it also means that
male Sparrowhawks fall comfortably within the size range
of the prey favoured by female Sparrowhawks and cannibalism
is not unknown, so the males need to exercise caution when
courting.

...as I was saying,
you're absolutely right,
dear. Again.

## KEEP STILL!

When a male Galapagos Tortoise (*Geochelone nigra*) is in the
mood for making love, it takes him a while to get into the
correct position. The female tortoise does not necessarily help
matters, sometimes choosing to wander off at the crucial
moment and obliging him to start all over again. To ensure his
paramour does not get away, the male resorts to rather
unsporting behaviour – he starts bashing her with his shell and
attacking her feet. Tiring of his shell-battering and the nips to
her toes, the female reacts by drawing her feet in and under her
shell to protect herself from attack. This also means that she is
no longer able to walk and the male has time to amble round
behind her and do his thing, which takes several hours and
involves much triumphant roaring.

## NO SEX PLEASE, WE'RE APHIDS

Who has time for that kind of shenanigans when you're intent on destroying someone's rose garden? Through the spring and summer, the female Rose Aphids or Greenfly (*Aphis rosae*) hatched that year reproduce by parthenogenesis, giving birth to a constant string of live genetic clones of themselves. This army of mini-mes grows at a phenomenal rate, the clones quickly maturing and spawning their own cloned babies. There may be 40 generations a year – and the unfortunate rose bushes are carpeted from stem to tip by plump, wingless, sap-sucking, constantly reproducing aphids. In autumn, the females start producing winged male and female babies, which don't feed but instead fly off to mate and lay eggs in a new rose garden, so the cycle can begin again next year.

# CHAPTER 7

# CHALLENGING CHILDCARE

Congratulations, you've made it to breeding age without being eaten by a predator and (if you belong to a sexually reproducing species) found a willing partner. There's just one more hurdle to cross now before you can really consider yourself a success at the game of life – passing on your genetic material. For those humans who choose to have children, the investment of time, energy and resources is huge. For some animals it's huge too, while others go for quantity over quality and spend no time at all on parental care, forcing the youngsters to fend for themselves right from the start. Then again, there are those that nurture their genes via a less direct route, by caring for siblings, nephews or other closely related kin. Animals are at their most vulnerable when they are young, and keeping them alive through these difficult times and preparing them for independent life is, for many species, the greatest challenge they'll ever face.

## PROCESS OF ELIMINATION

The Tasmanian Devil (*Sarcophilus harrisii*) is a 7kg, fierce, furry marsupial, which (like many species) has large numbers of babies to compensate for the fact that only the strongest few can survive. Those lucky few must prove themselves very early in life. Each newborn baby is just the size of a grain of rice and must crawl unaided from birth canal to pouch – a journey which requires extraordinary endurance and determination. Their predicament worsens, though, when the litter of up to 40 babies reaches the pouch and in it finds... four nipples. Only the first four that fix on to a nipple have a chance of making it to adulthood – for the rest, that arduous crawl to apparent safety was for nothing. Harsh.

## ALL SEWN UP

Many bird nests are stupendous constructions; they need to be, as they must house fragile eggs and chicks in shelter and safety for weeks or even months. Among the most inventive are those of the tailorbirds (genus *Orthotomus*). Finding a natural hollow in which to build a nest is a popular strategy among birds but natural hollows can be few and far between. Tailorbirds create their own, by fixing together two large, adjacent leaves along their sides and bottoms. The leaves are held together with stitchwork; the bird uses plant fibres or spider silk as thread and its own bill as a needle to pierce the leaves and draw the thread through. The nest proper is built inside this elegant leafy cup.

THIS NEST BELONGS TO: MR & MRS TAYLOR

## BODY MODIFICATION

Insects get up to some terrible things. Among the nastiest behaviour is that carried out by the parasitic wasps and flies, which inject their eggs into the body of a host caterpillar or other larger insect larva, which ends up being eaten from the inside out. One parasitic fly, *Compsilura concinnata*, injects living larvae rather than eggs, and those larvae have an unusual and gruesome solution to the problem faced by all internal parasite flies – they need to breathe and the host tries to stop them from breathing by coating them in melanin. To counter this, they actually cut out the poor host's own breathing tubes (tracheoles) and attach them to their own body pores.

## EGG PARTY

Ostriches (*Struthio camelus*) are polygynous, with one male courting a harem of up to seven females (and all the spare males presumably hoping for better luck next year). In the harem, one female is dominant and she is the first to lay her eggs, in a scraped-out hollow on the ground. The other females lay their eggs in there too afterwards, resulting in a large, mixed clutch. However, if there are too many eggs, the dominant female will kick out some of the peripheral ones (not her own, of course) to leave about 20 – a manageable clutch for one bird to incubate.

## EPIDURAL FOR MRS KIWI

As the biggest bird, the Ostrich lays the biggest egg of any bird, big enough to make an omelette for 10 hungry people, but in relation to body size it's actually the smallest. The biggest relative to size are laid by the small New Zealand relatives of the Ostrich, the kiwis (genus *Apteryx*). To give you the idea, a kiwi is about the size of a chicken but her egg is six times bigger than a chicken egg. To really give you the idea, google 'kiwi', 'egg' and 'x-ray' for some really eye-watering images.

Unsurprisingly, she lays just one egg a year, which takes about a month to develop in her body and the male kiwi lavishes great care upon it for the two or three months of incubation (though when it hatches the well-developed chick is quickly left to fend for itself).

## INSIDE MUMMY'S TUMMY

Swallowing one's offspring is not usually a good sign, but for the gastric-brooding frogs (genus *Rheobatrachus*) of Australia, there was no need to suspect foul play. The mother frogs swallowed their eggs soon after fertilization and the eggs released a chemical that caused the stomach to stop making hydrochloric acid and thus kept the eggs from being digested. After hatching out the tadpoles continued making the chemical. Meanwhile the mother frog did not eat at all and the tadpoles survived on the large yolk supplies that came with their eggs. Finally the mature froglets were unceremoniously puked up to begin independent life. If you're wondering why this account is in the past tense, it's because gastric-brooding frogs sadly went extinct in the 1980s.

*It's a boy!*

## BIG BAD BROTHER

Eagles might be our idea of the epitome of nobility but their behaviour in the nest is rather less gracious. The so-called 'Cain and Abel' situation occurs in many eagle species but is particularly well studied in Verreaux's Eagle (*Aquila verreauxii*) of Africa. Two eggs are laid a few days apart and thus hatch a few days apart. While the babies are still small, the larger chick invariably turns on the smaller, and after repeated vicious attacks eventually kills it, while the parents look on without intervening. This happens irrespective of how much prey the parents bring to the nest and there's much confusion as to why it occurs.

Um, yes, I was an only child too...

## BITE ME

Having children costs an arm and a leg if you're human. If you're a caecilian it will only cost you your skin. Caecilians (order Gymnophiona) are legless, worm-like amphibians which burrow through soil across the warmer parts of the world. The species *Boulengerula taitanus* is an egg-layer (some others give birth to live young) and when its eggs hatch the larvae use their frighteningly well-developed teeth to tear the skin off their (still very much alive) mother's body. The mother caecilian has grown an extra-thick layer of skin to provide for this and regrows the layer every three days so her babies can feast again.

## PREGNANT MALES

Kangaroos raise their young in pouches and so do seahorses (genus *Hippocampus*). The difference is that in the charming spiky-horse-shaped fish, it's the males who have the pouches. After a protracted day-long courtship, the female lays her eggs inside the male's brood pouch and he fertilizes them. The eggs hatch inside the pouch two or three weeks later and the male then gives birth, his body contracting strongly to push out up to 1,500 tiny babies. Parental care ends there, with the tiny fry setting off alone into the unknown. The seahorse couple, however, stay faithful to each other for subsequent couplings; the female even makes time to pay her mate a daily visit through all the long, tedious weeks of his pregnancies.

## BUILD YOUR OWN CRADLE

Caddisflies (order Tricoptera) lay their eggs in water and the parents are long dead by the time the babies hatch out. They must therefore look after themselves throughout the difficult months of infancy and they do this by building themselves a hardwearing case to live inside. The casing's foundation is made of silk secreted by the caddisfly larva but many species augment theirs with bits of debris found lying around on the riverbed, such as small stones, empty shells of water snails, sand and fragments of aquatic plants. Using natural materials like these, the larva provides itself with camouflage as well as a hiding place. As the larva grows, it modifies and extends its case accordingly and finally pupates inside it.

## LONGEST PERIOD OF PARENTAL CARE

*Longer-lived animals tend to invest more time into childcare. In social species, it can be impossible to determine when parental care stops and 'group membership' takes over. Orang-utans (Pongo pygmaeus), the least social great apes, care for their babies for five years. Frigatebird (genus Fregata) chicks depend on their parents for a full year, longer than any other bird.*

## ON THE TOAD'S BACK

The Surinam toads (genus *Pipa*) of South America are aquatic animals which look as though they have been trodden on, with their almost flat bodies. That broad back has an important job to do when it's time to breed: in the course of mating, the fertilized eggs are pressed on to the female's back by the male, and there they stay. A few days after mating is over, the eggs have sunk deep into her skin, each in its own little pocket. After hatching, the tadpoles stay in their respective pockets as they grow and develop, and don't leave until they are fully developed (albeit not fully grown) tiny toads.

## BABY BABYSITTER

For an example of brothers and sisters being much more decent to each other than eagles are, we can look to the White-rumped Swiftlet (*Aerodramus spodiopygius*) of Fiji. This fast-flying little bird builds a tiny cup nest, glued to a vertical surface such as a cliff or wall, and in this cup the female lays one egg, which she begins to incubate at once. A second egg is laid about two weeks later. By the time egg 2 has arrived, egg 1 has hatched, but unlike the older eagle sibling the newborn bears no ill will towards its relative but instead keeps the egg warm, effectively incubating it while its parents are away finding food.

## MASS DROP

Are you a fan of wildlife documentaries set in the Serengeti? If so, you'll be well aware that if there's any animal more likely to star in the 'being ripped apart by predators' role than an adult Blue Wildebeest (*Connochaetes taurinus*), it's a newborn baby Blue Wildebeest. To counter the highly catchable and eatable nature of their babies, Blue Wildebeests have evolved a breeding strategy whereby all the females in a herd give birth within two or three weeks of each other. This means it's party time for the predators like hyenas, which would not tackle an adult Blue Wildebeest, but the sheer glut of small calves around helps ensure that more of them survive to grow bigger, stronger and less easy prey.

And one, and two, and three, and GIVE BIRTH!

## MUM OF THE YEAR

There are many examples of exemplary maternal care throughout the animal world but not many of them are provided by insects. One insect group that does excel at mothering is the earwigs (order Dermaptera), who spend the best part of a year looking after their offspring. Male and female get together in autumn and live together in an underground chamber until late winter, when the female lays her eggs and evicts her live-in lover. She cares for the clutch of eggs over the next week, eating any mould that grows on them, turning them over and rearranging them, and fiercely driving off any would-be trespassers. When the eggs hatch, the new nymphs eat their eggshells and then live on food regurgitated for them by their mother. She continues to care for them until mid-summer (if she survives that long), whereupon they venture out in search of mates of their own.

---

### LARGEST CLUTCH OF BIRD EGGS

Gamebirds (order Galliformes) lay large clutches, with the Northern Bobwhite quail (Colinas virginianus) and Grey Partridge (Perdix perdix) producing up to 29 in a clutch. Baby gamebirds are independent soon after hatching. Tits (family Paridae), which feed and care for their chicks for several weeks, can produce 15 or more eggs in a clutch.

---

### FROM TREE TO SEA

Seabirds nest on cliffs. Or beaches. Or your roof, if you live in a seaside town. Marbled Murrelets (*Brachyramphus marmoratus*), however, nest in trees and, moreover, trees that are growing well inland and way above sea level. They are small seabirds, related to guillemots and puffins, and they nest on the branches of mature conifer trees in North American forests, with those that nest north of the treeline nesting on the ground. Like many small seabirds they are extremely vulnerable to attack from other birds when at the nest, which may have driven them to their unusual inland breeding grounds. The chicks grow up balanced precariously on a branch (well, it's not so different from balanced precariously on a cliff edge) and when they are fully grown they fly to the sea to begin their lives as proper seabirds.

## GONE PEAR-SHAPED

If you're making an omelette, it would be a mistake to leave the eggs lying around on the worktop while you fry the onions, because they'll roll off and smash. However, if you're using Guillemot (*Uria aalge*) eggs, this won't be a problem (though the resultant omelette may have an unpleasant fishy aftertaste). These cliff-nesting seabirds don't build nests but lay their eggs straight on to a narrow ledge. The eggs are shaped like symmetrical pears, with the round end very round and the pointy end very tapered. This way, if a Guillemot makes a less than textbook landing on its ledge and kicks the eggs, they won't roll off (usually) but will spin in a circle.

## HERMIT BABIES

Among the most appealing rock-pool animals are the hermit crabs (superfamily Paguroidea), soft-bodied crabs scuttling about in their odd assortment of borrowed mollusc shells. As hermit crabs grow, they have to wiggle out of the old shell before it's too late and swiftly find a larger replacement before a predator spots them. The Coconut Crab (*Birgus latro*) of the Indo-Pacific is a part-time hermit, living inside mollusc shells on the shoreline alongside other hermit crabs in its early months of life. As it grows, it finds fewer and fewer suitable shells and many switch to using broken coconut shells as temporary shelters. Before long, it is too big for even these, and its body begins to harden up as it reaches adulthood, making a protective shell unnecessary. By adulthood it is up to 40cm long, weighs more than 4kg and, as the largest land arthropod in the world, with an impressive set of claws, needs protection from no one.

## MIXED-SPECIES ADOPTION

Adoption in the wild animal world is quite unusual, even within the same species, so there was much interest in a lioness that chose to adopt a baby antelope. The large and handsome East African Oryx (*Oryx beisa*) regularly features on the Lion (*Panthera leo*) menu, but one particular lioness in a Kenya game reserve had other intentions when she approached a mother oryx and her calf. Scaring off the mother, the lioness 'adopted' the calf, keeping it close to her and guarding it from predators. She would allow it to return to its mother for milk but when the feed was over she chased off the mother and reclaimed the calf. The liaison ended abruptly two weeks later when a male lion killed the calf. However, the same lioness went on to adopt at least five more oryx calves before her disappearance in 2004.

## LIFE WITH THE ANTS

Ants are well known for 'milking' aphids of their sweet 'honeydew' secretions, defending the aphids against predators in exchange. Some caterpillars also produce honeydew, and in the blue butterfly genus *Phengaris*, an association with ants is a vital part of their lifecycle. Each caterpillar of the Large Blue (*P. arion*) of Europe spends a few days feeding on herbaceous vegetation, then drops to the ground. Here it is found by a red ant of the species *Myrmica sabuleti*, which strokes the caterpillar with its antennae, stimulating the secretion of a drop of honeydew. When this happens, the ant picks the caterpillar up and carries it off to the underground nest. There it lives among the ants and provides them with honeydew, in return feeding on ant eggs and larvae. It hibernates over winter and then pupates in the nest, emerging from the pupa in late spring. It makes its way out of the nest with a vigilant escort of ants fending off any predators and they guard it until its wings are fully dried and expanded and it's ready to fly away.

### LARGEST MAMMAL LITTER

*As we saw earlier, the Tasmanian Devil has a huge litter, as do some other related marsupials, but it is predetermined by the mother's nipple-count that only a few will survive. The largest litters of potentially survivable babies are born to the shrew-like Common or Tailless Tenrec (Tenrec ecaudatus) of Madagascar, with 30 surviving babies recorded from one litter.*

### THE COMPOST-HEAP CHICKS

Bird eggs need to be kept almost constantly warm to develop. Most birds accomplish this by sitting on them but a few have a different method. One such is the Australian Brush-turkey (*Alectura lathami*), which looks very turkeyesque but is in a different family. This species lives in groups, and each group nests communally, the females laying their eggs on a big mound of compostable material, which the group then covers up so the eggs are in the cosy heart of the heap. The males in the group guard the mound and adjust its height to ensure the temperature inside stays constant (they can test the temperature by thrusting their heat-sensitive bills into the mound). The newly hatched chicks dig their way out and go on their way, with no need for further parental care.

Nesting mound? No, this is just a perfectly natural hillock. Now, move along please.

### KIDNAPPED!

Penguins (family Spheniscidae) mostly live in large, dense colonies. Mother Emperor Penguins (*Aptenodytes forsteri*) leave their eggs in the care of their mates over winter and return in spring full of fish and maternal hormones, ready to lavish them upon the newborn baby. If there is no baby, due to some winter mishap, mothers will sometimes attempt to kidnap the offspring of a neighbour, though they seem to 'know' something is amiss and will abandon the kidnapped chick within a few hours or days. A male King Penguin (*Aptenodytes patagonicus*) was observed recently attempting to steal and care for the chick of a different species altogether, a Subantarctic Skua (*Stercorarius (antarctica) lonnbergi*). Ironically, adult skuas are voracious predators of King Penguin chicks.

## COOKING UP A BATCH OF BOYS

For most animals, sex is determined by which chromosomes you inherit from your parents. In crocodiles and some other reptiles, it's determined after conception, by the temperature at which the eggs are incubated (it's called temperature-dependent sex determination, or TSD for short). Mother crocs lay and bury their eggs in a hole dug in the river bank and guard them over several weeks of incubation. The baby crocs will be female if the temperature is on the cool or the hot side, with male babies only developing if the temperature hits a small window in between: in the Nile Crocodile (*Crocodilus niloticus*) it has to be between 31.7°C and 34.5°C. Females can influence this by the depth at which they bury their eggs.

## TOXIC PARENTING

There are lots of different ways parent animals can help keep their offspring safe from predators. One of the most ingenious is that employed by the slow lorises (genus *Nycticebus*), which are small and achingly cute and fluffy primates from southern Asia. These animals have venom-producing glands on their elbows and habitually lick up the venom so that they can deliver a more-than-averagely painful bite. When a mother loris has to leave her babies alone while she forages, she first gives them a thorough licking with her venomous saliva, so any predator to attack the baby will get poisoned. Since lorises usually only have one baby at a time, this method must be pretty effective at deterring any would-be predator before any damage is done.

## LOCKED IN

It's a nightmarish story straight out of one of those 'real-life' magazines. Boy meets girl, they fall in love, set up home together, boy impregnates girl... and a few days later she's been completely sealed up inside their home by a wall of clay. There's just a tiny hole left unplastered, through which he passes her morsels of food. For hornbills (family Bucerotidae) this isn't overprotectiveness gone mad but a perfectly normal and practical thing to do, and it is the female who does most of the plastering work (using fruit pulp and droppings as well as mud) to seal up her tree-hole nest. She incubates her eggs and nurtures the chicks in this ultra-safe nest chamber, while the male goes back and forth fetching food for his mate and offspring. In due course, the chicks are so big (and conditions in the nest, presumably, lacking a certain freshness) that no one is very comfortable anymore and the mother hornbill breaks down the wall to liberate them all.

and you NEVER see your kids... are you listening to me?

### LARGEST INSECT EGG

*Those laid by the Malaysian Stick Insect (Heteropteryx dilitata) are massive by insect standards, each the size of a whole grain of rice. They are also a peculiar, irregular shape to help disguise them from predators.*

## SEX DETERMINATION – THE NEXT LEVEL

If you thought what crocodiles do was clever, you'll be even more impressed by the control that Eastern Three-lined Skinks (*Bassiana duperreyi*) have over whether they have little boy skinks or little girl skinks. Like us, these Australian lizards have X and Y chromosomes, and XX means female, XY male. However, if the eggs are incubated at cooler temperatures, XX carriers develop with fully functional male bodies. And there's more – small eggs with a smaller quantity of yolk will tend to produce physically male lizards and large eggs with extra yolk produce females, regardless of chromosomes. So not only can this species produce XX males, it can also produce XY females. A mother skink therefore has two ways to potentially influence the sex of her babies – nest temperature and egg size – and there may be a third too, as some female lizards have been shown to be able to select which sperm fertilizes their eggs.

## A WOMB WITH A PLAN

Grey Seals (*Halichoerus grypus*) are superbly adapted to life in the water but there are some things that they can't do at sea, including mating, giving birth and suckling their babies. To save spending too much time on dry land, the seals mate as soon as their pups are weaned (when the pups are about four weeks old), and by the same time next year they are ready to give birth again, but there's a trick to this because the embryo only takes eight months to develop. The trick is delayed implantation. The fertilized egg spends three and a half months in suspended animation, just bobbing about inside the female's uterus. Then, when cues like day length indicate that the time is right, it implants and begins to develop and grow. This way, pups are born at the same time each year and the seals can get the tedious business of both sex and childcare out of the way in a quick four-week interval. Delayed implantation happens in many other mammals, enabling the females to give birth when conditions are just right.

## USURPER TO THE THRONE

A similar but even more exploitative brood-parasite strategy than that of birds like cuckoos is practised by certain insects – the so-called cuckoo-bees. Cuckoo-bees of the genus *Bombus* parasitize the nests of bumble-bees (also in *Bombus*) but use none of the guile that their avian namesakes employ. Instead, the egg-laden female cuckoo-bee enters the nest, finds the queen bumble-bee and does battle with her, often killing her. She then enslaves the workers in the nest, using a combination of pheromones and physical punishment to ensure they take care of her and her eggs. Once that brood has matured and departed, the mother cuckoo-bee goes off in search of another bumble-bee queendom to topple.

## CUCKOO IN THE NEST

Many species of cuckoo (family Cuculidae) are brood parasites, laying their eggs in the nests of other birds. The Common Cuckoo (*Cuculus canorus*) of Europe is a typical example. Although several small birds are popular hosts, each female specializes in a single species, and everything from her behaviour to the colour and pattern of her eggs is geared towards tricking that species. First she cases the joint, finding nests and assessing their state of progress. Then she waits until each nest is unattended (male cuckoos may help by distracting the parents) and swiftly lays her egg in the nest, before making off with one of the host eggs. The cuckoo egg develops and hatches quickly, and the baby cuckoo is strong enough to heft out the remaining host eggs (or chicks, if they have hatched), leaving it alone in the nest. The host parents apparently notice nothing untoward, even when the single baby has grown to three times their size and has an appetite that would shame a sumo wrestler.

He's got your face.

Oh yeah? Well, he's got your belly.

## SECOND CHILDHOOD

Many animals have distinct juvenile and adult body types. Only one, so far, has demonstrated the ability to change from adult to juvenile form as well as the other way round. This lucky creature is *Turritopsis nutricula*, a hydrozoan (jellyfish-like animal) which is found throughout the world's seas. The sexually mature form, a medusa or jellyfish, can revert to its colonial, sexually immature polyp form, back and forth theoretically forever. Being immortal has helped the species spread from its original Caribbean home to all tropical and temperate seas around the globe.

## WHEN'S IT DUE?

If you think nine months is an awfully long time to carry a baby, spare a thought for the Alpine Salamander (*Salamandra atra*). It is a long-lived amphibian, surviving up to ten years, but its pregnancies last up to three years. This is a result of living at very high altitudes (up to 1,700m), where the animal spends much of its time in an inactive, torpid state. At the end of the pregnancy two to four live babies are born. They are the survivors from a much larger crop of fertilized eggs; the other eggs provided sustenance to the survivors over the interminable gestation.

## MIDWIFE DAD

Frogs and toads certainly do exhibit an impressive range of parenting styles. With the midwife toads (genus *Alytes*), which are actually particularly warty frogs rather than true toads, the male takes charge of the fertilized eggs, which are produced in long strings. When fertilization is complete, the father winds the long, eggy strings around his belly and legs, and as they grow and swell, their father soon looks as though he has an unfortunate outbreak of boils about his nether regions. When the eggs are ready to hatch, the male finds a suitable pool and sits in it, waiting patiently until all the tadpoles have hatched out and swum away.

## COME FLY WITH ME

Baby birds don't need to learn to fly, it comes naturally. As soon as they are big and strong enough, they can just take off, though they quickly become more skilled at the finer details. Baby fruit bats (family Pteropodidae) get an extra advantage – they spend their early weeks hanging on to their mothers and get to experience flight as a passenger first. As fruit bats usually feed on fruit while perched, rather than anything more technically difficult, carrying a small baby around is not a great encumbrance. In due course the baby grows large enough to be left alone while the mother feeds and its next flight will be under its own steam.

## WE SUCK YOUNG BLOOD

We've covered a few examples of parents going to extraordinary lengths to protect and nurture their babies. In the case of the blind Madagascar ant *Amblypone silvestrii*, it's the other way round. When food supplies are short, the queen and workers in each colony sustain themselves by feeding on the haemolymph of the ant larvae – literally drinking the babies' blood – but not to the point that the larvae get sucked dry. This 'non-destructive cannibalism' has given the species the nickname 'Dracula ant', and the behaviour is thought to be a precursor to the food-sharing that takes place among other ant species.

Can't you kiss me goodnight without using your mandibles?

## DEATH TO THE FIRST-BORN

Killing one's offspring is a desperate act and animals generally only do it in desperate situations. Killing someone else's offspring, though, is another matter. When you are a male animal who's eager to pass on your genes, you will be less than delighted to meet a female animal who already has a batch of babies fathered by a different male. Under such circumstances, it's not at all unusual for the new male to kill the babies, in order to breed with the female himself. Male Lions (*Panthera leo*) are famous for committing infanticide. Another example was caught on CCTV in Scotland in 2007, when Loch Garten's regular male Osprey (*Pandion haliaetus*) returned late from his migration and found his mate was already incubating a clutch of eggs. Aware that he could not possibly have been involved, the angry bird of prey booted the whole clutch out of the nest.

## FASTEST MATURER

*Among mammals, baby Streaked Tenrecs (Hemicentetes semispinosus) move on to solid food as early as five days old, and females may be ready to breed just two and a half weeks later. Some quail species (genus Coturnix) can breed aged five weeks, while aphids are reproducing parthenogenetically after just one week of life.*

## BREATHABLE SKIN

Marsupial babies are born in a very underdeveloped state following very brief pregnancies compared with those of placental mammals. The pouch in which they spend their early lives is rather like a second womb. The newborn baby of the Julia Creek Dunnart (*Sminthopsis douglasi*), a delightful 'marsupial mouse', has an ability that is more often associated with amphibians – it can breathe through its bare skin. Over the first few days of its life it breathes with its lungs only occasionally, with the frequency increasing steadily as it grows. The skin-breathing can only work when the babies are tiny, with the largest amount of surface area relative to volume. Soon, their little lungs take over.

## LARGEST COMMUNAL NEST

*The Sociable Weaver (Philetairus socius) is a well-named bird, with pairs getting together to construct a huge haystack of a nest in a tree, which may contain as many as 100 nesting chambers. Other species of birds often share the structures as well.*

## TOUGH ENOUGH

Parents aren't supposed to have favourites among their offspring, and even if they do they must keep it to themselves to spare the feelings of the unfavoured (not to mention the ego of the one they like best). Not so for coots (genus *Fulica*). These water birds produce broods of about six but only a couple make it to adulthood and the parent coots are often the cause. They feed their favourites more, and less-favoured chicks are 'tousled', which sounds friendly but actually involves the parent grabbing the chick by its head and giving it a good shake. Many get 'tousled' to death. Some studies suggest that this is a test of resilience, others that the coots are actually attacking chicks that are not their own but came from eggs dumped in their nests by unrelated female coots which were 'caught short'.

## WHOSE NEST IS IT ANYWAY?

In southern Europe, there are two species of bird which like to build nests on or in buildings and use twigs and straw in their construction. One is the very big White Stork (*Ciconia ciconia*), the other the rather small Spanish Sparrow (*Passer hispaniolensis*). The stork's nest is a massive construction, piled up in a nice prominent spot (often the tower of the village church). Rather than go to the trouble of building their own nest, a pair of Spanish Sparrows will often 'sublet' a small part of the underside of a White Stork's, modifying it to create a suitable entrance hole and nest chamber. Many storks' nests contain numerous sparrow nests on their underside, an arrangement which has clear benefits for the sparrows and doesn't seem to bother the storks at all.

## MAN BOOBS

Why do males have nipples? And not only nipples but a small amount of mammary tissue underneath? In most species the nipples don't do an awful lot, they are just leftovers from before male hormones masculinized the female body template of the animal before it was born. However, in the Dyak fruit bat (*Dyacopterus spadiceus*) of South-east Asia, males can develop fully functional mammary glands and are thought to assist the females in feeding the young. No other mammal has so far been shown to possess this trait; in human males, for example, even the most impressive man boobs are purely ornamental.

I was hoping for something a bit more...masculine?

## DON'T SWALLOW

Where would a fish temporarily keep its valuables? In its mouth, of course. Many fish don't bother with parental care at all and compensate by producing vast quantities of eggs. However, several quite unrelated fish families have evolved the behaviour called 'mouth-brooding', whereby one or both parents take the fertilized eggs into their mouths and carry them around in there until the babies have hatched and are ready to go it alone. It's quite an inconvenience for the adult fish, who can't feed for the duration, but it does give each baby a much improved chance of survival and means the mother fish doesn't need to generate so many eggs.

## TEENAGE BABYSITTERS

Around ponds and lakes in summer, you'll often see Moorhens (*Gallinula chloropus*) tenderly feeding their ugly little babies on scraps of wet vegetation. Sometimes, the birds doing the feeding are not bright-billed, black-feathered adults but rather dull brownish-grey juveniles. These birds are too young to be the parents of the little ones they are feeding, so what is going on? The Moorhen is one of several birds in which youngsters from the first brood of the year will assist their parents in caring for subsequent broods. In doing so, they are not only helping their young siblings (who share 50 per cent of their genes) to survive but are also honing their own parenting skills for later in life.

## FROG IN YOUR POCKET

Australia is the land of things with pouches, as its mammals are almost all marsupials. By a strange coincidence, Australia is also home to a 'marsupial' frog – the Pouched Frog (*Assa darlingtoni*). This species mates and lays its eggs on land, unusually for a frog, and both parents stand guard over the eggs until they hatch. When they do, the mother's duties are over but the male has several weeks of childcare to go, as the tadpoles make their way into the remarkable pouches of skin on his sides. There they stay until they are fully developed.

## BUBBLING UNDER

Bubbles in water wouldn't be everyone's first choice for construction material, but if you're a fish, then bubbles have the distinct advantage of being easy to make. Various kinds of fish create floating 'bubble nests' in which to hide their eggs. A dash of sticky fish saliva makes the bubbles a bit more durable and in any case they are easily replaced. It is usually the male fish that makes the nest and he may begin making it before any spawning has occurred. Once he does spawn with a female, the eggs float upwards (or he carries them up in his mouth) into the mass of bubbles, and he guards them as they hatch and for some time afterwards.

---

### LONGEST PREGNANCY

*The surprise winner of this honour is a fish – the bizarre-looking Frilled Shark (Chlamydoselachus anguineus). It gives birth to up to 12 live young after an epic three-and-a-half-year pregnancy.*

---

## MAKESHIFT POUCH

The colugos (family Cynocephalidae) are among several mammal groups which have evolved the ability to glide, using a broad skin membrane (patagium) which stretches between their fore- and hindlimbs and between the hindlimbs and tail. The colugos have the largest patagia of any gliding mammal, and as well as making gliding possible, those folds of skin also make a cosy shelter for a baby colugo. The mother curls up her tail so the baby nestles inside the back section of the patagium as mum climbs about in the trees. When it's time for her to glide to a different tree, the baby hangs on to her underside for dear life as the patagium unfolds.

# CHAPTER 8

# DIETARY DELIGHTS

You could convincingly argue that no animal on earth has foraging and eating habits as strange as those of the average westernized human. Our ultra-convenient lifestyle does mean that the search and consumption of food takes up far less of our time than is the case for most animals, freeing us up to do other things like getting drunk, inventing world-improving or world-destroying technology, arguing, reading (and writing) books and so on. For many animals, the inventiveness, skill and courage involved in getting something to eat is quite mind-boggling to us, and feeding behaviour encompasses many of the things that make wild animals so fascinating and awe-inspiring to us. All the same, it may be as well to put down your sandwich before reading this chapter.

## SLIMED!

Velvet worms (phylum Onychophora) have cropped up a few times in this book because so much about them is weird. This includes their feeding behaviour: velvet worms snare their unfortunate prey – any invertebrate up to their own size – in a glob of sticky slime. The goo is generated in the animal's slime glands, located on the sides of the head, and can be fired a distance of about a centimetre. One squirt is enough to immobilize most prey, but large and vigorous prey may require some additional slime. The velvet worm then bites the prey to inject some saliva, which begins the digestive process. The prey plus the slime is consumed slowly and one meal lasts a week or more.

## BREAKING BONES

The Greek playwright Aeschylus is said to have suffered a most unusual death – legend has it he died after being struck on the head by a falling tortoise. Since tortoises are not noted for their powers of flight, a third party is presumed to have been involved, and the likeliest suspect is a Lammergeier (*Gypaetus barbatus*), a large and impressive vulture. Lammergeiers eat a lot of bone marrow, which they access by carrying the bone up to a great height, then dropping it on a rock to break it open – the same trick works with tortoises. Could a Lammergeier have mistaken Aeschylus's bald pate for a rock? Probably not but it does make a great story.

## FISH FARM

Cultivating plants to eat was one of the great human ideas that enabled us to take huge strides forward in our cultural development. It may, therefore, come as a surprise to learn that some species of fish are adept arable farmers too. Some damselfishes, which are related to the familiar colourful clownfishes and belong to the family Pomacentridae, cultivate algae for their consumption. The best studied is the species *Stegastes nigricans*, which finds and defends a fresh patch of a certain species of red algae. It 'gardens' the patch by removing other algae species; in its absence, other these interloping species quickly take over.

---

## MOST SERIOUS CROP PEST

There's no easy answer, as this varies from year to year as well as from country to country. Anything from elephants (genus *Loxodontia*) to thrips (order *Thysanoptera*) could be in the running. The Gypsy Moth (*Lymantria dispar*) is a ferociously invasive defoliator of trees, while the Colorado Beetle (*Leptinotarsa decemlineata*) historically caused utter devastation of potato crops.

---

## GIANT-KILLERS

The African Bush Elephant (*Loxodonta africana*) is the mightiest land animal and should fear no other beast. The elephants of Savute in Botswana, however, can't sleep so easily at nights, for the local Lions (*Panthera leo*) specialize in taking on this most impressive prey. Across Africa, different lion prides tend to favour particular prey. In Savute, where droughts can be severe and prolonged, one huge pride of up to 50 lions regularly kills elephants, often juvenile males but sometimes full-grown adults. The lions select a straggler in the group and always attack from behind, jumping on the elephant's back or flanks but staying out of reach of trunk and tusks. When the giant finally topples, the lions have a feast that can last days. The rest of the elephant group rarely attempt to intervene; in particular, adult bulls seem suspiciously indifferent to the fate of their younger rivals-to-be.

## ISOPOD GOT YOUR TONGUE?

It looks like an albino woodlouse but *Cymothoa exigua* is a much more sinister beast. It is a marine isopod crustacean that lives off the coast of California and parasitizes the Spotted Rose Snapper fish (*Lutjanus guttatus*) in a most unusual manner. It gains access to the interior of the fish via its gills, then makes its way to the tongue, biting into the base and thus firmly attaching itself to the host. Over time, the parasite drains the tongue of blood, and eventually the tongue withers away and *Cymothoa exigua* functionally replaces it. Yes, the poor fish now has to use the parasite as a tongue, while the parasite continues to live on the host's blood and/or mucus from other fish the snapper eats.

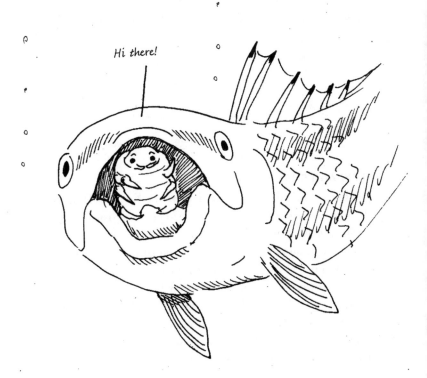

## HUNGRIEST ANIMAL

*Not for nothing did Eric Carle write of a Very Hungry Caterpillar in the much-loved children's book. The caterpillar of the Polyphemus moth (Antheraea polyphemus) is an eater extraordinaire, putting away 86,000 times its own weight in tree leaves in the two months between hatching and pupating.*

That was a nice breakfast. Now it's time for lunch.

## SLOW AND SURE

The biggest lizards on Earth today are the Komodo Dragons (*Varanus komodoensis*) of Indonesia. These are truly fearsome beasts, reaching 3m in length and more than capable of killing and eating a human. Although Komodo Dragons have been found to possess venom glands, the venom is thought not to play a substantial role in the way they kill their prey. Of more significance is the incredible concentration of virulent bacteria in their saliva. If an ambushed deer, for example, manages to escape a dragon attack with just minor nibbling, it is still doomed even if it quickly puts miles between itself and its attacker. The bacteria soon take hold and the deer will slowly become more and more unwell. Meanwhile, the dragon's excellent sense of smell will enable it to track down the injured deer and be ready to step in when the infection renders its prey totally incapable of another escape attempt.

## A TOUGH NUT TO CRACK

The Brazil nut. It's many people's favourite in the Christmas nut bowl but you need a strong grip and skill with the nutcracker to access the kernel from its hard and angular casing. In its natural state, this nut is even more well protected. It falls from the tree in the form of a large, round, coconut-like fruit with a thick, woody shell. Inside this are up to 24 of the familiar irregularly shaped nuts, arranged in a circle like the segments of an orange. Only one animal is naturally equipped to penetrate the Brazil nut fruit. The Brazilian or Red-rumped Agouti (*Dasyprocta leporina*) is a large, ginger-furred rodent which, like all rodents, has strong gnawing incisors. It chews its way into the Brazil fruit to get at the nuts, eating some straight away and burying others for later. Some of the latter get forgotten and germinate into new Brazil nut trees, meaning that the agouti is responsible for ensuring the spread and survival of its favourite tree.

## INSIDE OUT

Resembling a fat marine worm drenched in slime, the hagfish (family Myxinidae) is an unprepossessing creature indeed. It is an opportunistic predator, capable of attacking sea creatures much larger than itself, especially if the victim is injured or otherwise compromised. The hagfish bites a hole in its prey and then squirms inside, eating it from the inside out. Fishermen bringing up a net from the seabed have often found their catch to be full of hagfish, all enthusiastically devouring the more desirable fish.

## BLEEDING DELICIOUS

If you find bats a bit creepy, look away now. The vampire bats (subfamily Desmodontinae) comprise three species, all living in South, Central and the far south of North America, and they all drink the blood of other animals – birds in the case of two species. The third and most notorious species, the Common Vampire Bat (*Desmodus rotundus*) attacks mostly mammals and will happily include humans among them if it gets the chance. It walks and runs swiftly for a bat and will scramble over its victim in search of a good spot to bite (it has heat-detecting sensory cells on its nose to find where there's a good supply of blood close to the victim's skin surface). The bite is painless, rarely waking the victim, and the bat laps rather than sucks blood from the wound. An anticoagulant compound in its saliva keeps the blood flowing for as long as required (and for a little while afterwards, but not enough to harm the victim). The biggest risk from a vampire bat bite is not death by blood loss but catching rabies.

But I thought you were a 'Twilight' fan!

## PLAYING DEAD

Corpses don't last long in the water. Many aquatic animals are quick to take advantage of a free meal and small fish waste no time in gobbling up any dead animal they happen to find. Livingstone's Cichlid (*Nimbochromis livingstonii*) is a fish of Lake Malawi in Africa that takes advantage of this behaviour. Its patterning is an irregular marbling, like that of a fish which has begun to decay. When hunting, it lies motionless on its side on the lake bed, pretending to be a tasty cadaver. When a curious little fish approaches, the 'corpse' comes back to life at lightning speed, dashing at and seizing its victim.

## THE MONKEY HUNT

Common Chimpanzees (*Pan troglodytes*) are, like the other great apes, primarily vegetarian. However, they enjoy a bit of meat with their veg now and then, especially in the dry season, when plant matter is less available and appetising, and have various clever ways of obtaining it. The most famous is the hunt for Western Red Colobus monkeys (*Piliocolobus badius*), whereby groups of chimps pursue their quarry through the tree-tops and any kills are shared by the whole group. Chimps have also been observed fashioning spears from branches, using their teeth to sharpen one end to a point and then stabbing the spear into tree holes to extract sleeping galagos (family Galagidae).

## SINISTER SECRET

Most people in the UK know the Great Tit (*Parus major*) well – it's the colourful, chirpy, cheeky chappie with the black head and white cheeks that does acrobatics for peanuts on the garden birdfeeder. But there is a dark side to this inventive little bird. It has been found to occasionally attack something much larger, furrier and more alive than peanuts – hibernating pipistrelle bats (genus *Pipistrellus*). When the sleepy bats wake in their communal roost in early spring and start to squeak dozily to each other, their calls attract the Great Tits, which come in and attack the more-or-less helpless little mammals, pecking at their skulls to remove their brains. The behaviour has only been observed at a particular bat roost in Hungary, suggesting that it may have been invented by one local Great Tit and then imitated by others.

## SWEET TEETH

Plants, being rooted to the spot, often use the services of animals to move pollen from flower to flower. The pollinating animal receives payment for its services in the form of nectar. Most animal pollinators are insects, but of those that are not, one of the most surprising is the Kinkajou (*Potos flavus*). This mammal is a medium-sized, long-tailed, tawny-coloured relative of raccoons and lives mainly in Central and South America. Although it comes from a family of carnivores it eats mostly fruit and enjoys nectar, which it extracts using its very long tongue. As it feeds, pollen sticks to its face and is subsequently transferred to new flowers. However, the Kinkajou does sometimes spoil this harmonious plant–mammal association by eating the flowers whole.

## BATTY FOR BIRDS

We've seen that little birds may eat little bats – and the reverse is true as well. Many small songbirds migrate at night, to avoid the attention of day-flying bird-killers like hawks and falcons. The Greater Noctule bat (*Nyctalus lasiopterus*) lives in southern Europe and is an adept hunter of birds; it is the only bat species to habitually catch birds in flight. It is a fast and manoeuvrable flyer, and its echo-location squeaks are pitched above the hearing range of most birds, so they can't hear it coming. In summer it feeds mainly on insects, like related bat species, but it takes full advantage of the many migrant birds passing through its territory in spring and autumn.

## COLOUR ME BEAUTIFUL

If you're wondering why your pet flamingo has lost its lovely pink colour and become a boring off-white, the answer is in its diet. Foods can affect the colour of the animal that eats them – with flamingos, live brine shrimps help supply the pink feather pigment. The yellow face of the Egyptian Vulture (*Neophron percnopterus*) is enhanced by regular consumption of cow dung. Individuals with deeper yellow faces do better with the opposite sex, so this is a literal example of successful seduction being helped along with plenty of bovine excrement.

## A PIECE OF YOU

The biggest shark teeth relative to body size belong to a very small, 50cm shark with an interesting name. The Cookiecutter Shark (*Isistius brasiliensis*) lives in deep, warm seas and has bioluminescence that camouflages it in the scattered natural light that reaches the deeper water. Around its neck is a collar of dark skin that lacks light-producing photophores, and to

other fish this dark patch is the only visible part of the Cookiecutter. Mistaking the dark bit for a silhouetted small fish, other fish attack the Cookiecutter, whereupon it turns the tables and bites them. Its round mouth and big sharp teeth leave a characteristic circular wound in the victim. Because its attacks rarely kill its much larger victims, it is often classed as a parasite rather than a predator.

---

### FASTEST FEEDER

*Frogfish of the family Antennariidae are slow and sluggish bottom-dwelling sea fish, but when prey strays too close to them they can suck it into their mouths in just six milliseconds, faster than any other animal and too fast for the human eye to register what just happened.*

---

### PIRATES OF THE HIGH SEAS

Many seabirds are superb fishers, securing their prey from a dramatic plunge dive from the air or swimming to impressive depths in a long chase. Other seabirds are much better at flying than swimming and sometimes use this to their advantage to steal fish from the hard-working swimmers. The most noted birds to indulge in this so-called kleptoparasitism are the skuas (family Stercorariidae) and the frigatebirds (genus *Fregata*). Both intercept their victim as the latter is flying from sea to land with a bellyful of fish intended for its own chicks, and chase and harry it until the unfortunate bird can take no more and vomits up its catch.

### SILICON AND CHIPS?

Sea sponges (phylum Porifera) are peculiar beasts. Quite a few of them have tiny silicate spines incorporated in their cells,

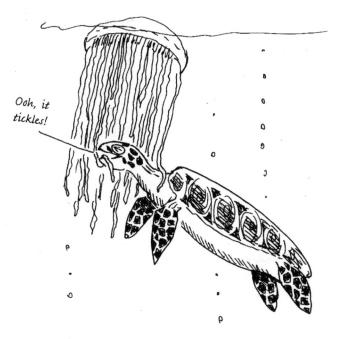

Ooh, it tickles!

which form a skeleton-like lattice. This makes them rather inedible to other sea animals, as they are, essentially, made of glass. One animal that does seem quite happy to munch them by the glassy mouthful is the Hawksbill Turtle (*Eretmochelys imbricata*). This tough customer not only relishes the silica-based sponges but also eats many species that contain potent toxins, and when not tucking into a sponge supper, the Hawksbill also feeds on that deadliest of jellyfish, the Portuguese Man o' War (*Physalia physalis*). It closes its eyes when it consumes this prey; no other part of its body is vulnerable to the Man o' War's stinging tentacles.

### GLUG, GLUG, GLUG

Camels (genus *Camelus*) are famous for being able to survive extended periods without drinking. However, when the opportunity arises, they are also capable of swigging down extraordinary volumes of the stuff in next to no time. Both the mono-humped Dromedary (*Camelus dromedarius*) and the two-humped Bactrian Camel (*Camelus bactrianus*) are reputed to be able to take on board more than 100 litres of water in a single drink. Unlike other mammals, their red blood cells are oval rather than circular, which makes them stronger and less likely to rupture when all this fluid suddenly enters their systems.

## SPIT IN YOUR FACE

Frogs and lizards are famously accurate at catching insects by firing out their long, sticky-tipped tongues. The Archer Fish (*Toxotes jaculator*) of Asia and Australia performs an even more impressive feat to capture prey that's resting on overhanging foliage well above the water's surface. It takes in a mouthful of water and then tilts its body upwards and lets loose a high-speed water cannon at its target, knocking the insect off its perch and into the water, where the archer quickly gulps it down. An Archer Fish with a few years' experience under its belt can hit an insect that's 1.5m away and even take out a flying target.

## CAVIAR EVERY DAY

Most sea snakes (family Hydrophiidae) are venomous and make their living by hunting and eating fish. The Spine-tailed or Marbled Sea Snake (*Aipysurus eydouxii*) of Australia is one of a few species that has taken a different path in life and feeds almost exclusively on fish eggs. These snakes have specialized scales around their mouths for digging up eggs or scraping them from rocks. They have also almost completely lost their venom glands, along with most of their teeth.

## A POO DIET

Eucalyptus leaves are rubbish as a foodstuff. They contain lots of toxins and hardly any nutrients, so it's not surprising that few animals will eat them. The one we all know that does is the Koala (*Phascolarctos cinereus*) of Australia and it has a super-efficient liver to detoxify its diet. It also has a very long caecum (part of the colon), full of bacteria which help ferment the leaves to extract maximum nutrition from them. Baby Koalas lack the bacteria, so in between feeding on mother's milk and graduating to a leafy diet, they feed on a soft runny substance called 'pap' (but it would be just as accurate to call it 'poo'). Excreted by the mother, this contains all the bacteria the baby needs to set up its own caecal colony of fermenting bacteria.

## THE BRAIN-EATERS

Red Imported Fire Ants (*Solenopsis invicta*) from South America are fierce little critters, currently causing a problem as an introduced species in North America, but they are vulnerable to a species much smaller than themselves. Flies of the genus *Pseudacteon* parasitize the ants in the most gruesome way. The female fly lays an egg in the ant's thorax and the larva migrates to the ant's head, where it slowly devours all the contents. The ant can continue to live a (sort of) normal life for a while, thanks to subsidiary 'mini-brains' (ganglia) elsewhere in its body, but after a couple of weeks it has abandoned its ant-duties entirely and is wandering about like a zombie. The fly larva ends the ant's misery by releasing an enzyme that dissolves the connection between head and body, whereupon the ant's head drops off and the fly larva pupates inside.

---

## MOST POWERFUL PREDATOR

*The largest hunter on earth is the Sperm Whale (Physeter macrocephalus), which regularly tangles with the hugest squid species. Predators that single-handedly tackle prey much larger than themselves include the Stoat (Mustela erminea), which hunts Rabbits (Oryctolagus cuniculus) up to ten times its size.*

---

## TAKING THE WIGGLE OUT OF THE WORM

You're a Mole (*Talca europaea*) and you eat lots of earthworms. However, there are always those times when you're out digging a new bit of burrow and you're not at all hungry but you find a very tasty-looking worm. What to do? Keep it for later of course, but how to stop it squirming away? Like several other mammals of the order Soricomorpha, Moles have a venomous bite, and they use it to paralyse prey so that they don't have to eat it straight away but can stash it in the Mole equivalent of a store cupboard for later.

## DRIED OUT

Birds help waterproof their feathers by greasing them down with an oily goo that's secreted from a gland under the rump feathers. This oil permits the famed rolling of water off a duck's back, without seeping through and chilling the bird's body. Cormorants (genus *Phalacrocorax*) have water-permeable outer feathers, which may help them to swim underwater more quickly. While the water doesn't reach the birds' soft underfeathers, it does mean the long feathers of wings and tail get wet and weighed down after a dive, so cormorants are obliged to spend some time post-dive standing around with their wings open to help dry them out.

### SKIMMING THE SURFACE

Perhaps the strangest-looking bird bills of all belong to the skimmers (genus *Rynchops*). From the neck down, they are very attractive and graceful-looking birds, like supersized terns with long wings and great agility in flight. Attach to this body an oversized head and a bizarre, huge carrot of a bill with the lower jaw (mandible) much bigger and longer than the upper one and, voilà, that is a skimmer. To feed, it flies along low above the water, with its head drooping downwards, its bill open and the oversized lower mandible trailing in the surface of the water, seizing floating prey items as it goes.

## MORE THAN YOU CAN CHEW

Among animals that swallow their prey whole, there are several cases of individuals taking on prey too big for them, with lethal consequences. One gruesome example was a Perentie (*Varanus giganteus*), an Australian monitor lizard, which tried to swallow a Short-beaked Echidna (*Tachyglossus aculeatus*), aka Spiny Anteater. Those spines fatally pierced the lizard as it struggled to engulf its bulky prey. Another ill-advised eating attempt would delight Wile E. Coyote – a Roadrunner (*Geococcyx californicus*) found dead with a gruesomely split neck in Texas after trying and failing to swallow a Texas horned lizard (*Phrynosoma cornutum*).

I'm going to swallow you whole!

Well...if you say so...

## BLOOD-SUCKING BIRD

The most remarkable of Darwin's finches is probably the subspecies *Geospiza difficilis septentrionalis*, or 'Vampire finch', which lives on Wolf and Darwin Islands in the Galapagos. It is one of the sharper-billed of the finches, and while it mostly feeds on seeds and insects, it also uses that pointy beak to peck holes in the toes of unsuspecting seabirds called boobies (genus *Sula*) and drink their blood. As if that weren't enough, the finch also sometimes steals newly laid booby eggs, rolls them away and breaks them against rocks to consume the contents.

---

## MOST AMBITIOUS EATER

*The Black Swallower (Chiasmodon niger) is a little-known deep-sea fish which habitually swallows fish larger than itself – up to twice as long and ten times heavier. If it doesn't digest the prey fast enough, decomposition sets in, which kills the Black Swallower and floats its body to the surface, which is how we know about its amazing appetite.*

---

## THE SUBTERRANEAN FROG

Plenty of frogs bury themselves in the ground, whether to hibernate or to shelter temporarily. Only one lives an almost permanent underground existence, the Purple Burrowing Frog (*Nasikabatrachus sahyadrensis*) of India, and it lives there because that's where its prey is. It feeds on termites and lives among their network of tunnels, taking advantage of the moist and well-ventilated soil conditions the termites produce. The frog has tiny eyes, as it hardly needs to see down there, and a pointed nose tip for probing tunnel walls in search of the next mouthful of termites. Oh, yes, and it's purple.

## FITTING THE BILL

You can make a fair guess about what a bird likes to eat by looking at the shape of its bill. Delicate pointy bill = insect-eater, strong conical bill = seed-cracker, sharp, hooked bill = meat-eater and so on. There are a few birds out there with really unusual bills, used to exploit unusual food sources. Take the Wrybill (*Anarhynchus frontalis*) of New Zealand, a plover with a bill that bends to one side (usually the right). The shape is handy for flipping over stones to find little critters beneath. The spoonbills (genus *Platalea*) are tall, heron-like birds with long, flattened bills that widen at the end like a ladle; they sweep the open bill from side to side in the water, snapping up any small invertebrates that touch the bill sides. The Spoon-billed Sandpiper (*Eurynorhynchus pygmeus*) of Russia is a much smaller, unrelated bird with a similar bill shape and feeding style.

# CHAPTER 9

# STRANGE SOCIETY

Some animals, like some people, just don't get on with others of their kind and lead a solitary existence, except when it's necessary to get together for a brief and tension-filled liaison for breeding purposes. Others spend their entire lives, from cradle to grave, in the company of their family, extended family or just a great gathering of others of their species. Social (and antisocial) behaviour among animals is especially intriguing to us humans, as we can see something of our own ways in them – after all we, like many other primates, have highly complex and well-developed social behaviour ourselves. This chapter is all about how animal social groups function together, how social interactions help build and break relationships, how different species sometimes work together for the benefit of both parties, and what happens when it all goes wrong.

## YOU WORK FOR ME NOW

The slavemaker ants (genus *Epymyrma*) show distinctly antisocial behaviour in their bid to take over the ant world. Ravoux's Slavemaker Ant (*Epimyrma ravouxi*) of France is a typical example. The queen gains access to other ant nests by feigning death, whereupon the workers carry her into their nest, probably intending to eat her. Once inside, she drops the act and engages the resident queen in battle, killing her. Now, rather gruesomely, she clothes herself in the carapace of the dead queen, fooling the nest of workers that nothing untoward has occurred, and the workers continue as usual, unaware that they are now serving an alien queen.

## PILED VELVET

It's back to the wonderful world of velvet worms (phylum Onychophora) again, this time for a look at their social lives. As we saw in chapter 8, velvet worms are predators, spitting gluey slime at their prey to immobilize it. Because they can capture quite large prey this way, velvet worms often live and hunt in groups, wolf-style. Each group is led by a dominant female, who feeds first whether she made the kill or not. Any insubordination is subdued by chasing and biting the miscreant, and dominant animals often climb on to the backs of their subordinates to assert their position. On the other hand, juveniles never chase and bite others but will climb on top of them, perhaps to avoid trouble.

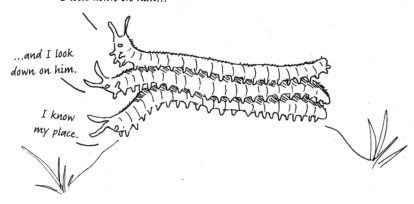

I look down on him...

...and I look down on him.

I know my place.

## THE ODD TRIO

Great Nicobar Island in the Indian Ocean is home to a variety of exotic wildlife, including a tree-climbing, insectivorous mammal, the Nicobar Tree-shrew (*Tupaia nicobarica*); various small hawks, including the Nicobar Sparrowhawk (*Accipiter butleri*); and a shiny black, insect-eating bird, the Racket-tailed Drongo (*Dicrurus paradiseus*). It's recently been observed that tree-shrew, hawk and drongo have a bizarre cooperative association, despite the fact that the hawk would be quite capable of preying on either of the other two. The drongo finds the tree-shrew and follows it as it forages, seizing insects that it disturbs. The hawk looks for the drongo in order to find the tree-shrew, and it too is there to catch insects or larger animals that are disturbed by the tree-shrew. The tree-shrew itself benefits from the vigilance of the two birds and their ability to drive off potential predators. It's an uneasy alliance but one that seems to work for the three disparate animals involved.

---

## LARGEST INSECT GATHERING

Various non-biting midges (families Chaoboridae and Chironomidae) form huge swarms over Lake Victoria in Uganda when billions of billions (really) of adults emerge for their short-lived breeding orgy under each month's full moon. Local people take full advantage of them by making batches of squashed-fly burgers when the swarms are around.

---

## WHO'D BE A LION?

It's well known that in Lion (*Panthera leo*) prides, the females do all the hunting but then have to step aside to let the males eat first. Females also have to suffer the loss of their cubs when new males take over the pack and kill all the small babies. Overall, however, the life of a male Lion is harder than that of a lioness. On average, the males of a pride will only manage three years there before they are ousted by other, stronger (or more numerous) males. Paranoia about when the next takeover attempt is coming leads to males often spending long nights patrolling their territorial boundaries, roaring loudly to try and deter any nearby males. Confrontations are often fiercely violent, and ageing males have no chance of maintaining a position within any pride. While old females are supported by their female relatives and may live to be 15 or more, old males are forced to live alone and rarely survive beyond 12.

## TEAM HARRIS

If ever there was an enduring image of a solo hunter, it's the bird of prey, cruising alone through an empty sky for vast distances and scanning the ground far below for something to swoop at. There are some social birds of prey, though, including the Harris Hawk (*Parabuteo unicinctus*) of North America, which hunts as a pack. It is very accomplished at this, using several different strategies to secure its prey. The group of about five birds may attack simultaneously from different directions or pursue in a relay, with a new bird attacking if the first should fail. Sometimes one hawk will flush out a hiding rabbit by chasing it on foot into the open where the other hawks are waiting.

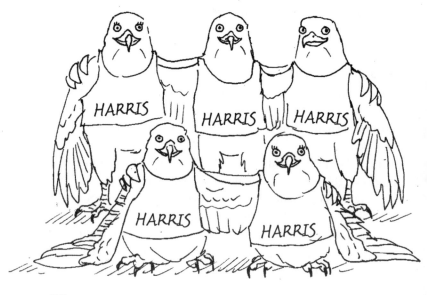

## SNAKE!

If you've ever been on safari in the wilder parts of southern Africa, you'll know the Vervet Monkey (*Chlorocebus pygerythrus*) well, as the cheeky git who'll steal all your food given a moment's opportunity. These clever monkeys are much preyed upon by eagles, snakes and Leopards (*Panthera parda*) and when one of these predators approaches, a quick and appropriate response is necessary. Therefore, the monkeys learn from infancy three distinct and different alarm calls for the three predator types. If a monkey gives the 'eagle' call, the others check the sky while hurrying to the safety of nearby bushes. If it's the 'leopard' call they take to the trees, where their agility will keep them safe from the big cat. The 'snake' call provokes a reaction of standing up on the hind legs and searching the ground.

## THE ULTIMATE SACRIFICE

Worker ants and bees are never going to breed, so all their energies go into protecting their colony and the one or a few individuals within it that do reproduce. It's well known that worker honey bees will die after using their stings, a sacrifice well made if they succeed in deterring a dangerous intruder. Another social insect, the Asian termite *Globitermes sulphurous*, also self-destructs for the greater good. Soldiers of this species will, if unable to fend off an attacker with bites, release a sticky goo from a gland on their necks. In really dire straits, the glands will actually rupture in an explosion of goo, killing the termite but unleashing enough goo hopefully to block the path of the intruder.

## QUEEN RAT

Loose, wrinkly, hairless skin, tiny useless eyes and huge, projecting, gnawing incisors. It's not a recipe for beauty but it works for the Naked Mole-rat (*Heterocephalus glaber*), a

You will meet me in my bedchamber this eventide.

burrowing rodent of East Africa. Naked Mole Rats live in social groups which are structured like bee or ant colonies. One dominant female breeds, mating with two or three favoured males, and all the other animals in each colony – up to 300 individuals – are non-breeding workers, extending the group's tunnel network or guarding it from intruders. There is only one other mammal which lives in a so-called 'eusocial' arrangement like this – it is another, slightly less unattractive species of mole-rat.

## YOU AND ME AGAINST THE WORLD

Monogamy in mammals for a breeding season is quite rare and a pair teaming up for a life-long liaison is even rarer. A shining example of this way of life comes from the elephant shrews or sengis (family Macroscelididae) of Africa – small, cute fuzzies with rather long and flexible noses. They pair for life, the female having several litters a year, and work together defending a territory from other elephant shrews. If the challenger is male, the male of the resident pair is the one to drive him off, while the female deals with female intruders.

## BAND OF BROTHERS

The luckiest male Cheetah (*Acinonyx jubatus*) is the one who has brothers, because these speedy cats do best when they work as a team. If a male Cheetah has no brothers, he may team up with other lone males if he finds any, though nearly half of all adult male Cheetahs are solitary. A male's chances of success in securing a territory, hunting well and fathering babies are much improved if he lives in a small coalition with one or two other males. The females live alone, although mothers, daughters and sisters are tolerant of each other and their home ranges often overlap, with males seeking to establish their territories at these points of intersection.

### MOST NUMEROUS BIRD

*The Red-billed Quelea (Quelea quelea) is a small seedeater from Africa, with a population of about 1.5 billion.*

## NEMO OR NEMETTA?

The Disney–Pixar film *Finding Nemo* is a charming tale of a father clownfish searching for his last surviving son after the death of his wife and other children but it was not without a few biological errors. Firstly, clownfish (in the subfamily Amphiprioninae) live in groups, rather than in human-style family units, with a dominant female in charge and doing all the breeding. Secondly, they are sequential hermaphrodites. This means that to be true to the realities of the natural world, when the mother clownfish died in the film the father should have changed sex in order to become the new dominant female of the group. With this system, every fish in the group, whatever its sex, may eventually get its chance to be top of the heap.

203

## FAIR PLAY

The human sense of justice and fairness for all is well developed and, when it is offended, can cause us to behave in some rather peculiar ways. Testing whether Chimpanzees (*Pan troglodytes*) shared this trait, researchers trained a group of the apes to perform a certain task and rewarded them with a slice of cucumber if they succeeded. All well and good, but when some of the chimps were given a more desirable reward of a grape instead, those that were offered cucumber slices spurned them and refused to continue to work. Brown Capuchin monkeys (*Cebus apella*), social animals which are known to be clever and adaptable, showed a similar 'toys out of pram' response to unfair treatment in a similar study.

## MOST SPECIES-RICH PART OF THE WORLD

*In general, there is most biodiversity close to the equator, with numbers of species falling as you get closer to the poles. The Atlantic Forest of Brazil is perhaps the world's most significant 'biodiversity hotspot', with 950 species of bird, millions of insects and similar wealth in all other land animal groups.*

## UNEQUAL PARTNERSHIP

It's one of the classic examples of animal symbiosis – the industrious, bright-billed little oxpeckers (genus *Buphagus*) busily picking ticks and lice from the hides of large grazing animals on the African plains. Food for the bird, no more annoying skin parasites for the mammal – what could possibly go wrong? The trouble is that oxpeckers don't just like ticks and lice. They also like dead skin and blood, and have been shown to keep wounds open on their unfortunate hosts. Also, they prefer to eat ticks that have already drunk their fill of blood from the host. Moreover, a study in Zimbabwe on domestic cattle showed that those that received oxpecker visits were just as tick-ridden as those to which oxpeckers were denied access. On the other hand, oxpeckers eat earwax, which may be of real benefit to their hosts. It's quite possible that for some species of large mammal oxpeckers are a good thing, while for others they're an absolute menace – in the words of academics everywhere, further study is needed.

## THE CUSTOMER IS ALWAYS RIGHT

When a sea fish is feeling a bit crusty and itchy, it will stop off at a cleaning station to have its dead scales and any external parasites removed by the cleaning squad. Cleaner wrasses (genus *Labroides*) attract the attention of passing trade by gathering at specific spots and wiggling about in an eye-catching manner. Sometimes, a cleaner wrasse will take liberties and eat some of the client's vital skin mucus – a better meal for the cleaner but this is not acceptable to the client, who rapidly leaves in a strop. The perpetrator of the 'mucus theft' is then treated aggressively by other cleaners, for selfish behaviour by one cleaner can result in reduced feeding opportunities for the whole group.

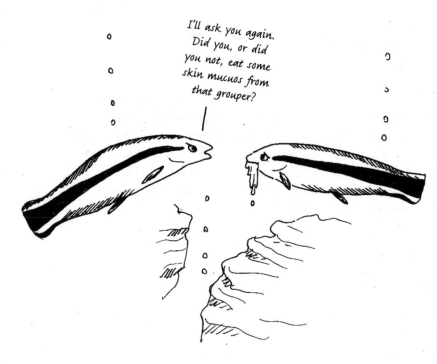

## JOINING THE ARMY

If you're on your first birdwatching trip in South America, you'll probably be quite bewildered by the variety of species described in your field guide. You may also notice that an awful lot of them have 'ant' in their names; there are ant-pittas, ant-thrushes, ant-wrens and plain old ant-birds. Why all the ants? Many of these birds spend a lot of their time following the moving phalanxes of army ants (genus *Eciton*). As the ants storm through the forest, jumping on and killing any insect or other small animal that's too slow to get away, the birds are there to hoover up those that do escape the ants. Up to 30 different bird species may be in attendance to an army ant swarm, with possibly hundreds of individuals.

## CATCH ME IF YOU CAN

Perhaps the most intriguing communication that occurs among animals is that between a predator and the prey animal it's trying to catch. Often, an animal that's being pursued will try to convince its attacker to give up the chase by flaunting its physical fitness, as if to say 'Try an easier victim; you don't stand a chance of catching me.' Gazelles (genus *Gazella*) and some deer perform a very high four-legged jump for this purpose, a behaviour called 'pronking' or 'stotting' (though sadly not 'boinging'). Predators will avoid the highest pronkers. Male Skylarks (*Alauda arvensis*) may mock pursuing Merlins (*Falco columbarius*) by singing while they are being chased; the falcons give up chasing singing Skylarks much faster than ones that stay silent.

## PUTTING THE NEMO IN THE ANEMONE

The other thing clownfish are famed for is their association with sea anemones (order Actiniaria). Sea anemones are predators, trapping passing fish and other creatures in their stinging tentacles. However, clownfish are immune to the stings. They therefore can shelter within the tentacles when danger threatens, and they assist the anemone by gobbling up potentially harmful invertebrates in its vicinity, as well as providing it with extra nutrition in the form of plenty of clownfish poo.

## PRAIRIE TALK...

Because we know monkeys are clever, it's not that surprising to learn that Vervet Monkeys have a kind of language. When it comes to the prairie dog (genus *Cynomys*) of North America, however, the range and sophistication of its linguistic abilities is truly remarkable. The prairie dog is a chunky little burrowing ground squirrel, tasty eating for Coyotes (*Canis latrans*), American Badgers (*Taxidea taxus*) and other predators. It lives in tight-knit social groups, and group members warn each other of danger with a series of high, sharp, barking calls, which all sound the same to the average human. However, analysis of the wave patterns of calls show they vary according to the predator involved, and playback of the calls to the prairie dog colony produces the appropriate search response for that particular predator.

PRAIRIE DOG

Good morning!
Ee! Ee! Ee! Ee!

Lovely weather today.
Ee! Ee! Ee! Ee!

Are coyotes a big problem
for you here?
Ee! Ee! Ee! Ee!

I don't think that the
government does enough.
Ee! Ee! Ee! Ee!

PHRASE BOOK

We had a wonderful time
in Paraguay.
Ee! Ee! Ee! Ee!

No, we booked the car
hire separately.
Ee! Ee! Ee! Ee!

They don't have a coyote
problem at all.
Ee! Ee! Ee! Ee!

And there's lots to see.
Ee! Ee! Ee! Ee!

## STRONGEST FAMILY TIES

*Many animals stay in family groups for life. The elephants (genus Loxodontia) are perhaps those that show most devotion to their female-led groups, tending to the ill or injured and showing distinct signs of grief and mourning over their dead.*

## ... AND THE PREDATORS' REPLY

So the Prairie Dogs have a social defence against Coyote and American Badger attacks. The two predators sometimes counter this by joining forces when they hunt Prairie Dogs and other ground squirrels. Unlike many other dog species, Coyotes are not pack-hunting animals; they do live in family groups but tend to hunt alone. However, it's quite common to see a Coyote hunting alongside an American Badger, and those that do enjoy better hunting success. Although both dog and badger are hoping to make a kill and will not share it with their 'partner' if they do, their different hunting styles (overground pursuit for the Coyote, chasing the prey underground for the badger) mean their competition is indirect. And working together to find and flush out prey means each has more opportunities than either would if they were alone.

## A LOAD OF CROCS

What's more alarming than one Nile Crocodile (*Crocodylus nilotecus*)? Lots of them, hunting as a team. Although they usually hunt alone, Nile Crocodiles will join forces at certain times, most spectacularly when intercepting the mass migration of one or other of Africa's large herbivorous mammals. As the zebras or wildebeests surge across the water, one croc will attack a selected animal, and if the strike is successful others will join in to quickly subdue the prey. The team continues to hunt until the migrating herd has passed through and only then will they feast on their kills. Crocs have also been seen forming a 'living dam' to block the path of migrating fish.

## PUTTING ON A SHOW

We've all seen those natural history films in which schools of fish twist and turn with amazing synchronicity, looking like a shimmering wall of light. What's the point of all that showing off? One key function is to confuse and disorientate predators, who find it hard to home in on a single individual when the whole shoal is moving as one. A similar phenomenon can be seen in flocks of Starlings (*Sturnus vulgaris*), which fly over their roost sites in spectacular swirling, rippling flocks. Much research is underway to work out how the school or flock moves with such synchronicity; it seems likely that each individual strives to maintain the same position in relation to those immediately around it, so a 'group consensus' is in operation.

## MERLIN? WHAT MERLIN?

Predators have their own ways of tricking their prey, too. Most small songbirds are quick to spot an approaching bird of prey and raise the alarm – the flight style of a hawk or falcon is highly distinctive. Most bird-hunting raptors use natural cover to sneak up on their prey. Sparrowhawks (*Accipiter nisus*) will fly ahead of cars on narrow roads to pounce on flushed birds. Merlins (*Falco columbarius*), which are relatively small falcons, can evade detection by copying the flight style of a much more innocuous bird to get close to their intended prey. They abandon their usual fast, flickering flight and use a lazy, bounding, thrush-like action to fool their victims and get close enough for a sure-fire attack.

---

## MOST NUMEROUS MAMMAL

*Leaving aside nearly 7 billion humans, there are more Crabeater Seals (Lobodon carcinophagus) on Earth than any other large wild mammal, with a population of up to 50 million (all in Antarctica). Very common small mammals like House Mice (Mus musculus) and Brown Rats (Rattus norvegicus) probably number in the low billions worldwide, though making accurate assessments is almost impossible.*

---

## SMELLING DINNER

Very young ladybird larvae (family Coccinellidae) need to find food fast if they are going to make it to their first moult and they locate it by smell. Studies have shown, though, that the larvae aren't drawn to the smell of their aphid prey itself but to the smell of squashed aphids, in other words to the aphids' alarm pheromones. This smell strongly suggests that there is another ladybird larva nearby, tucking into an aphid lunch. By scrounging a share of an older, larger larva's meal rather than trying to manage a whole aphid on its own, the younger larva greatly improves its chances of survival.

## ARMED GUARD

Eusociality, where a colony of animals has only one or a few breeders and a much larger proportion of non-breeding workers, has been noted in several animal groups beyond the familiar quartet of wasps, bees, ants and termites. One intriguing example comes from the Caribbean Sea, where the pistol shrimp *Synalpheus regalis* lives in colonies inside sponges. One female is mother to the whole colony, which includes a high proportion of 'soldier' males with one enlarged claw, which snaps with a pistol-like crack when the shrimp is really annoyed with another sea animal. This shrimp is the first marine creature found to show eusociality, though it probably won't be the last.

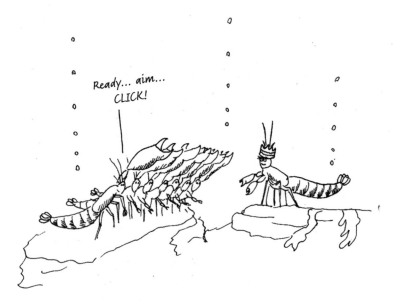

Ready... aim... CLICK!

## BIRDS OF VARIOUS FEATHERS

In the spectacular Sinharaja forest of Sri Lanka, the morning calls of the Greater Racket-tailed Drongo (*Dicrurus paradiseus*) are the signals for a variety of birds to get together and start

the day's foraging. This is the place where the largest and most diverse mixed-species foraging flocks on Earth can be seen, but variations on the same theme occur throughout the world. The flocks are strongly associated with woodland habitats, and contain mostly songbirds (order Passeriformes). There are several advantages of feeding in moving groups like this. More eyes mean more concentrations of insects will be found and predators are more likely to be detected.

# CHAPTER 10

# HARASSING HUMANITY

Long ago, when our ancestors roamed the plains and hadn't done much about inventing wheels or discovering fire, there were two kinds of animals – the ones you could eat and the ones that could eat you (and, probably, a few that fitted either category, depending what time of day it was and how many spears and friends you had with you at the time). As we developed our culture and found ways to place distance between ourselves and the messy immediacy of kill-or-be-killed, we began to appreciate other attributes of these animals and to start to notice the other life forms around us. There were the ones that were too small to be worth eating but looked good on a headdress, the ones whose venom-secreting skins could be used to anoint arrowheads, the ones whose fur could keep us warm. Then there were the animals that we could make better use of if we kept them alive, to supply eggs and milk, to be ridden, to guard us and to provide us with company. From horses to bees, and wolves to ducks, the list of animals successfully domesticated is a long one, and continues to grow to this day. Despite this growing empathy, we were mostly still interested in killing animals and turning their habitat into landscapes more suited to our own needs. Now, the tide is starting to turn and many human cultures are backpedalling hard to reverse damage to wildlife habitats and to restore the populations of those animals we've brought close to extinction. Human–animal relations, in short, have had a turbulent history. Here we look at some of the more interesting outcomes of when man meets beast.

## BREAKERS' YARD

There are quicker ways to disfigure a car but few are as entertaining as this. In the mountainous parts of South Island, New Zealand, there lives a rowdy tribe of parrots which specialize in biting bits off cars. The Kea (*Nestor notabilis*) is a clever green parrot with a large and very serviceable bill, which it uses to demolish almost anything it encounters. Park your car at a South Island ski resort at your peril, for the Keas suffer from extreme neophilia (love of 'new things') and in their curiosity will gnaw and worry at any loose object they can find, meaning that you may well return to a car that's now missing its aerial, windscreen wipers and door seals.

### LONGEST AND SHORTEST SCIENTIFIC NAMES

*Proving that entomologists are gluttons for punishment, the longest scientific name bestowed on an animal belongs to a fly – Parastratiosphecomyia stratiosphecomyioides. At the other extreme is the Great Evening Bat – Ia io.*

## CROSS CATS

If you want a pet exotic big cat but consider both Lions (*Panthera leo*) and Tigers (*Panthera tigris*) too small and weedy for your needs, the only other option is a Liger. As there is now no overlap between the wild ranges of the two parent species, the only way to produce this hybrid is in captivity. Pairing a male Lion with a tigress results in a litter of Ligers, which will grow up to be considerably larger than both parents. The reverse mating of male Tiger with a lioness produces Tigons, which are smaller than their parents. Sadly, both hybrids are susceptible to assorted congenital health problems and are usually sterile.

## PARROT FASHION

Dr Dolittle wanted to converse with animals of all kinds and so do we. It's long been known that some bird species are able to mimic the human voice accurately, but whether this goes beyond simple imitation is a matter of speculation. One example of what seems to be real understanding between bird and human was provided by an African Grey Parrot (*Psittacus erithacus*) called Alex. His handler reported that Alex, who knew about 100 words, could understand simple abstract concepts, recognize several shapes and colours, and invent portmanteau words (for example, on seeing his first apple, he dubbed it a 'banerry' – a combination of 'banana' and 'cherry' – two fruits with which he was already familiar).

## THE MAN-EATERS OF TSAVO

The Hippopotamus (*Hippopotamus amphibius*) might be the most dangerous large animal in Africa but there's a chilling difference between killing someone because they annoyed you and killing someone because you want to eat them, which is why most of us find Lions (*Panthera leo*) that bit more worrying than Hippos. The famous man-eaters of Tsavo were a couple of rogue males who showed just how scary Lions can be during their reign of terror in 1898. At the time, workers were constructing the railway line between Kenya and Uganda, and the two Lions started attacking the workers in their tents at night. About 35 men died before the Lions were eventually tracked down and killed, each mighty animal absorbing several bullets before finally giving up the ghost.

## SIGNED UP

The vocal apparatus of Chimpanzees (*Pan troglodytes*) and Gorillas (*Gorilla gorilla*) is such that making the complex sounds of human speech would be very difficult for them. However, individuals of both species have been taught to use sign language and have shown impressive communication skills. The most famous signing ape is a female Gorilla named Koko, who can use about 1,000 signs and can also understand some 2,000 words of spoken English. Both she and a signing Chimpanzee called Nim Chimpsky are credited with forming simple sentences. Nim's longest utterance was the rather jumbled but emphatically meaningful 'Give orange me give eat orange me eat orange give me eat orange give me you.'

## ANIMAL PET-KEEPERS

One quality Koko the Gorilla shares with many humans is a love of domestic cats. She adopted her first kitten in 1984 after asking her trainer for a cat. She chose a grey kitten, gave him the name 'All-ball' and treated him with great tenderness and affection. She expressed distress and sorrow when he was accidentally run over and went on to adopt other cats. Interestingly, she always chose tailless Manx kittens for her pets, perhaps because of her own tailless physique. Another captive female Gorilla, Toto, also adopted a kitten in the 1930s, showing the softer side of an ape species which, at the time, was much feared and reviled, thanks to the rather misleading film *King Kong*.

---

### MOST DEADLY ANIMAL

*Hippos are more dangerous than lions, and bears, crocs and sharks have all gone some way to earning their terrible reputation. However, the animal responsible for the most human deaths is the malaria-carrying mosquito (genus Anopheles) – malaria kills about a million people a year.*

---

### OLD BLUE AND THE EGG-SWAPPERS

The dramatic 11th-hour rescue of the Chatham Island Robin (*Petroica traversi*) from extinction is a triumph of cooperation between man and bird, though of course the bird was only doing what comes naturally. One of just five of her species remaining, the robin Old Blue was also half of the only successful breeding pair and was already a senior citizen in bird years (she was nine) when conservationists got involved. To keep Old Blue laying eggs, the conservationists moved her clutches to the nests of another common songbird species, which acted as foster parents. Today, the population of the robins has recovered to about 250 birds, all descended from Old Blue and her mate.

### CLONING LIKE RABBITS

Ever since Dolly the sheep, cloning animals has been a hot topic in biology. Using the technology to boost numbers of endangered species has always been one of the favourite and less controversial possible applications. In Japan, scientists have used it to create a new embryo from the dead body of an Amami Rabbit (*Pentalagus furnessi*), a dark-furred, small-eared bunny that occurs only on two tiny islands. However, even if cloning proves to be a realistic way of increasing the stock of Amami Rabbits, the main problem of habitat loss still needs to be resolved if the species is to prosper in the wild.

## THE HARRODS LION

It's hard to imagine that less than 50 years ago you could pop into Harrods and come out with a Lion cub (*Panthera leo*). In 1969 Australians John Rendall and Anthony 'Ace' Bourke did just that and kept the cub, Christian, in a London flat, until his increasing size made this impractical. They contacted well-known Kenya-based conservationist George Adamson, who took on Christian and integrated him into a wild pride. The cub's original owners went to Kenya to visit him in 1972, unsure whether the young animal would remember them. He did and the joyful reunion was captured on film. Today it is one of the most popular video clips on YouTube.

## A CUP OF SPECIAL COFFEE

If you already think coffee is disgusting, you probably won't be tempted to try a nice refreshing mug of Kopi Luwak, aka 'Civet coffee'. The beans used to make this beverage are special in that they have completed a full transit through the digestive tract of an Asian Palm Civet (*Paradoxurus hermaphroditus*), a mongoose-like animal native to southern Asia. Civets are not to be confused with either weasels or cats, although they are sometimes called 'civet-cats'. The civet eats the coffee 'berries' and digests their pulpy outer layers but the beans inside emerge intact. However, the animal's digestive enzymes do penetrate to some extent and enhance the flavour of coffee brewed from the beans; it is apparently a smoother and less bitter drink. Kopi Luwak from wild-collected beans commands a frighteningly high price, although captive civets are now being used for a more efficient harvesting process.

Mmm, it's so smooth!

You should have seen it yesterday...

## I NAMED IT AFTER YOU

The names people have given to animals over the years provide a rich hunting ground for oddness. One of the commonest trends, prevalent in the 18th and 19th centuries, was for naturalists to name newly discovered species after other naturalists, perhaps hoping the favour would be returned. The Italian naturalist Alberto della Marmora commemorated his colleague Francesco Cetti by naming a warbler after him. Mr Cetti is generously referenced in both the bird's English name and scientific name (twice) – Cetti's Warbler (*Cettia cetti*), which some might consider overkill. Marmora himself lives on in a warbler's name too, though only its English name – Marmora's Warbler (*Sylvia sarda*).

## OF LICE AND MEN

One of the advantages of hairlessness is that there are fewer places for external parasites to hide on our bodies. We do suffer from attacks from two different kinds of hair-loving lice, though – *Pediculus humanus* (the 'head louse') and *Phthirus pubis* (the 'pubic louse'). You may have noticed that the two species have different genus names, indicating they are not closely related. While head lice seem to have adapted along with their human hosts and are quite unlike other lice infesting different animal species, the human pubic louse bears a suspiciously close resemblance to lice found on Gorillas (*Gorilla gorilla*). It's been theorized that our ancestors sneakily slept in empty gorilla nests, thus picking up the parasites; it's certainly a more feasible (and more palatable) idea than the alternative.

## THE BIKE-HATING BUZZARD

Cyclists around Holsworthy in Devon were advised never to forget their helmets in the early 2000s as a local Common Buzzard (*Buteo buteo*) developed a passionate hatred for the lycra-clad pedallers. In a spate of overzealous territorial rage, the raptor attacked more than 20 cyclists before the traffic fought back; the bird was reported to be killed by a van in 2004. However, either this was a case of mistaken identity or a different buzzard has since taken over – another cyclist was whacked on the head in 2007.

## SPOT THE DIFFERENCE

Like many animals that we have domesticated over the years, dogs have diversified into a dazzling array of shapes, sizes, fur lengths and coat colours. One of the most immediately recognizable breeds is the Dalmatian – a dapper, medium-sized short-hair with black or brown spots scattered across its white coat. That spotty gene has an unfortunate side effect though – a tendency to accumulate uric acid in its body. Other dog breeds (and in fact other mammals) can convert uric acid into a second substance, which is easily excretable, but in Dalmatians the acid crystallizes into painful bladder stones. It's not unlike gout in humans, except that with us the uric acid crystals are formed in our joints, producing an arthritis-like pain.

## DELICIOUS – AND NEW TO SCIENCE

The discovery of a species hitherto unknown to science is the ultimate goal of many a naturalist, and even today with so much of our world mapped out in tremendous detail, such discoveries are still being made, often in unexpected ways. One such find took place in the mountains of Tanzania in 1991. A strange pair of feet discovered protruding from a villager's cooking pot were found, on further analysis, to belong to a new species of bird, which has since been named the Udzungwa Forest-partridge (*Xenoperdix udzungwensis*). The species has now been seen alive and well in the wild and is classed as endangered – but that's because it has a small population in a vulnerable area, not because too many of them have been eaten.

## DOORSTEP DESTRUCTION

Given our long tradition of putting out food for the birds, we can hardly blame said birds for assuming anything edible left outside is there for them. It was only a few decades ago that everyone had a doorstep delivery of milk, which came in glass bottles sealed with a foil lid. Most of this milk was 'full fat', with the creamiest portion forming a visible layer in the top quarter. Those enterprising garden birds, the tits (family Paridae), worked out that the foil lid was easy to peck through, giving access to lovely creamy milk. Now milk deliveries are uncommon, the tits have yet to learn how to go to Tesco and buy their own, but it's surely only a matter of time.

Oh great. What about my cornflakes?

## WAR HEROES

Animals have played crucial roles in wartime for many nations. In Britain, outstandingly heroic animals are awarded the Dickin Medal to honour their work. A total of 54 animals received the medal for their gallantry during World War II – 32 pigeons, 18 dogs, 3 horses and 1 cat. Since then, eight more dogs have joined the honours list. The pigeons won their medals for message-carrying missions, the dogs for various search-and-rescue and bomb-locating feats and the horses were police horses working the beat in London during the Blitz. As for the cat, he dealt with a rat infestation on board the Royal Navy sloop HMS *Amethyst*, despite sustaining gunfire injuries.

## PUPPET PARENTS

Around the world, people are working to improve the population and situation of many endangered species and using many clever and inventive techniques to help achieve this. The California Condor (*Gymnogyps californianus*), a dramatic and huge vulture-like bird, had declined so much by the late 1980s that its entire wild population (just 22 birds) was captured for captive breeding. Many of the eggs laid were hatched in incubators and the chicks hand-reared. Food was given to them using condor-shaped hand-puppets, so the chicks imprinted upon the right species, and in due course some were returned to the wild and bred successfully. The wild population has now reached nearly 200 individuals.

Dad, why do you never smile? And why do you smell of rubber?

## WORKING BIRDS

Why bother waiting in your boat for something to take your bait when you can send an expert swimmer in to chase down a fish supper for you? Fishermen in parts of Japan and China enlist the help of cormorants (genus *Phalacrocorax*) – large, ungainly water birds that are adept pursuit hunters of fish. It might be possible to tame a cormorant but apparently it's more difficult to train it to deliver its catch to you rather than swallowing it, so working cormorants have a rope tied around their throats to prevent them from swallowing all but the smallest fish.

### MOST NUMEROUS DOMESTIC ANIMAL

There are more chickens in the world than there are people – far more, in fact, with some 50 billion of them reared every year. The other popular farm animals – cows, sheep and pigs – number a billion each or thereabouts. Pet cats and dogs number about 500 million and 400 million worldwide, respectively.

## UNFORESEEN CONSEQUENCES

The three large vulture species of India (genus *Gyps*) have an important role in the lives of rural people. Not only do they deal with the carcasses of deceased livestock but also, for followers of the Parsi faith, they are undertakers for the human dead. At least, that used to be the case. But the 40 million vultures in India in the early 1980s has now plummeted to just 60,000, after a mystery ailment struck and seemed to sweep through the vulture population at terrifying speed. In the early 2000s the cause of their deaths was discovered – not a virulent disease but an anti-inflammatory drug used to treat cattle. Diclofenac was accumulating in the vultures' bodies and giving them kidney failure. The drug is now banned but is still widely used and a recommended replacement has proved toxic to the birds as well. The only hope now for these critically endangered birds is probably a captive-breeding programme, so a stock of birds can be established for release into the wild once the risks to the birds can be eliminated or greatly reduced.

## AN EYE FOR AN OWL

Being a bird photographer sounds like a pleasant way to make a living, if you can manage it. The well-known photographer Eric Hosking must have had mixed feelings on the subject; he achieved fame and acclaim only after he lost an eye to a violently camera-shy Tawny Owl (*Strix aluco*). In north-east Europe, the related Ural Owl (*Strix uralensis*) looks like a giant, pale and, if anything, more benign version of the Tawny but is rightly feared for its aggressive character. Ornithologists fixing leg rings on baby Ural Owls need to take with them a couple of accomplices armed with branches, to fend off the repeated violent attacks of the mother owl. The Swedes call this species 'Slaguggla', meaning 'strike owl'.

## CAN A CANDIRU?

Of all the awful animal tales out there, the one of the candiru fish (family Trichomycteridae) of the Amazon River is one of the most blood-chilling. Rumour has it that the tiny, skinny fish is drawn to the smell of urine when a bathing human has a sneaky pee, and it swims up the urethra and lodges there, held in place by its spiny gills as it feeds on the poor victim's blood. The candiru is indeed a parasite, but studies have shown that, while it is strongly attracted to the smell of blood, it is indifferent to the scent of urine. Even so, it would be wise to cover up any open wounds and wear protective coverings over all orifices, however small, before bathing in candiru-infested waters.

## SLAVE, MAKE MY BREAKFAST

*Whaah!*

A recent study showed that cat owners are better educated than dog owners. This seems somewhat at odds with the results of another study, which revealed that domestic cats have adapted to exploit and manipulate their owners in a rather clever way. Happy cats purr but cats who want something from their humans give a special, high-frequency purr which hits the same trigger in the human brain as a baby's cry. We are ill-adapted to ignore the cry of a baby, and the 'food-soliciting purr' of a cat gnaws at our senses in just the same way, ensuring we quickly stop what we are doing and go and top up the crunchies bowl.

## LEADING THE WAY

The hand-puppet technique used with California Condors has also been used in the USA with captive-bred Whooping Cranes (*Grus americana*). An additional problem with these birds is that they are migratory, with youngsters learning the correct route by following their parents and other adults. The captive-bred cranes were trained to follow ultra-light aircraft instead and only needed to be shown the outward route once; they proved capable of making their own way back after the first time. The conservationists have even used this technique to teach some cranes a new, safer route to the wintering grounds.

## A FRIEND WHO UNDERSTANDS

Humans are predisposed from a very early age to study and scrutinize other human faces. When we look at someone else, we tend to look mostly at the right side of their face, as this more reliably reveals the emotions currently being experienced by the owner of the face. Now, research has shown that pet dogs have a similar right-hand bias when studying a human face. They don't show it when looking at images of dogs' faces though, just people, suggesting that they have learned how best to read a human's emotional state.

---

## MOST VENOMOUS ANIMAL

*Forget snakes, spiders and frogs. The worst of the lot are (probably) the box jellyfish (class Cubozoa), especially Chironex fleckeri, which carries enough venom to take out 60 people.*

---

## GIVEN THE CANE

People have, over the centuries, found many reasons for letting loose non-native animals in various parts of the world. Sometimes they have done it simply because the animal in question is nice to look at and they fancied having it around. That was not the case with the Cane Toad (*Bufo marinus*), a large, grim-looking and extremely toxic amphibian from Central and South America, which was introduced to many other countries in the 19th and 20th centuries. The plan was that the toad would gobble up the beetles and other insects that were devastating crops. It didn't really work out. In Australia, the Cane Toads had little impact on the sugar cane-eating beetles as the fields offered insufficient shelter for them. However, they have run rampant among the fragile native Australian fauna, eating the small stuff and poisoning to death any large creatures that try to eat them. Eradicating the toads seems to be impossible now but preventing their further spread is a top priority for conservationists in Australia. Meanwhile, carnivorous marsupials such as quolls are learning to avoid this poisonous prey.

## LIKE A HEADLESS CHICKEN

One autumn day in 1945 a Colorado farmer chose a rooster for the family supper and chopped its head off with an axe. His aim was a little off though, and while the bird's head as we would recognize it was indeed severed, most of its brainstem was intact, as was one ear, and a blood clot in the carotid artery saved the bird from death by blood loss. When the headless rooster continued to run around for a lot longer than you'd reasonably expect, the farmer realized that it was still very much alive, and instead of becoming that night's roast dinner, 'Mike' the headless chicken became a much-loved and famous pet. His family put food directly into his exposed oesophagus and kept his trachea clear of mucous. He was quite able to strut and hop around, though his rooster crow was little more than a gurgle. Many admirers visited Mike over the next 18 months, until he sadly choked to death one night.

Do you fancy going for a run around?

*gurgle*

## ALIEN NATION

Visit any park in England and you'll probably be accosted by a Grey Squirrel (*Sciurus carolinensis*), seeking nuts. Over in the States, it's equally easy to encounter House Sparrows (*Passer domesticus*) – the species is often called the 'English Sparrow' there to reflect its origins. Thanks to humans, England is full of American squirrels and America is full of English sparrows, and our unfortunate habit of bringing animals from one part of the world to another has had numerous problematic consequences for the native animals of the land. With the Grey Squirrels came a disease deadly to our native Red Squirrels (*Sciurus vulgaris*), while over in the USA the House Sparrows are vigorously outcompeting native birds like the Eastern Bluebird (*Sialia sialis*) and Purple Martin (*Progne subis*) for nest sites.

## PEOPLE AND PANDAS

The Giant Panda (*Ailuropoda melanoleuca*) is one of the most recognizable and popular animals on Earth. It's also in deep trouble, thanks to loss of its forest habitat in China. To boost its numbers, conservationists have been trying to breed pandas in captivity for many years but it's an uphill struggle as males and females seem quite disinterested in each other in the captive state. Giving the males Viagra and showing panda couples some exciting 'panda porn' of mating pairs had limited success. Now, artificial insemination is working well to boost the captive panda population, although ensuring the safety of the animals in the wild is a whole separate battle.

## DO YOU TAKE THIS GOAT...?

When a Sudanese man was caught in a compromising position with his neighbour's female goat in 2006, the village elders decreed that the perpetrator should pay the goat's owner a dowry, as he had 'used it as his wife' – effectively, he was forced to marry the goat. The story caused widespread amusement but is not the only recorded case of human–animal marriage. Other documented cases include marriage to dogs, horses, a snake and a dolphin.

## GENTLE GIANT

Every so often there's a news story concerning someone who decides to join a large and dangerous zoo animal in its enclosure, usually with gruesome results. For a refreshing change, consider the case of Jambo the Gorilla (*Gorilla gorilla*), who resided at the Jersey Zoo from 1972 until his death in 1992. In 1986 a five-year-old boy fell into the Gorillas' enclosure at the zoo, knocking himself unconscious. Jambo, the head of the Gorilla group at the time, took charge of the situation, standing guard over the boy and stroking his back, not allowing the other curious Gorillas to come near. When the boy woke up and began to cry, an alarmed Jambo backed off, enabling keepers to enter the enclosure and extract the boy.

Someone call Social Services!

## PACK IT IN

In the UK, a person with an overriding desire to collect objects, especially shiny ones, might be called a 'magpie' after the similarly bling-loving bird. In the US, a likelier nickname is 'packrat', after the Bushy-tailed Woodrat (*Neotoma cinerea*) or one of its close relatives – the so-called packrats. They are medium-sized rodents, with cute big ears and wide eyes, which makes them rather more attractive to look at than the average rat. When they come into people's homes, though, they are a real nuisance, thanks to their compulsion to collect any stuff they find lying around and take it away to decorate their large and very cluttered and untidy nest chambers – aka 'middens' (which also serve as toilets). Analysis of middens can be valuable for archaeologists, as all the packrat pee dries out and crystallizes to form a sturdy vault, which preserves the stuff inside (often including things stolen from human habitations of the time) for up to 40,000 years.

## CRYPTOCATS

Out on the fringes of biological study is cryptozoology – the study of animals which may not exist. It includes Bigfoot, Nessie and other never-observed creatures but also covers the possible continued existence of apparently extinct animals and the rumoured presence of well-known living species far away from where they are supposed to be. In the UK, everyone's favourite example of a cryptozoological mystery is the existence, or not, of big cats roaming our countryside. Most of the eyewitness accounts concern 'black panthers', which is a bit odd in itself as melanistic big cats are not common in the wild or in zoos. And most of the photographic evidence shows black domestic cats. However, there is quite a bit of real evidence that there are some big cats at large out there, probably illegal pets that were released by their thoughtless owners. We just need a conclusive photo or video clip—

## DEGREES OF OUCH

One can only wonder about the mental state of the entomologist Justin O. Schmidt when he decided to create a 'sting index' ranking the painfulness of various different bee, wasp and ant stings – from his own experience. The 'Schmidt Sting Pain Index' now ranks the stings of 78 species on a scale of 1 to 4 and describes the stings in poetic detail. For example, that of the Bullhorn Acacia Ant (*Pseudomyrmex ferruginea*), ranked 1.8, is 'A rare, piercing, elevated sort of pain. Someone has fired a staple into your cheek.' Top of the stings with a full 4 is the redoubtable Bullet Ant (*Paraponera clavata*) – 'Pure, intense, brilliant pain. Like fire-walking over flaming charcoal with a 3-inch rusty nail in your heel.'

## LONGEST-LIVED PET

*A Radiated Tortoise (Astrochelys radiata) from Madagascar, presented to the royal family of Tonga in either 1773 or 1777 lived until 1965, making it 188 or 192 years old. One pet Sulphur-crested Cockatoo (Cacatua galerita) reached 100 years of age. A handful of domestic cats have reached their mid-30s, while the oldest dog died aged 29 and a half.*

# FURTHER READING

Whether you'd rather browse the web or go to the library, there's no shortage of accessible and more in-depth technical reference material on the amazing lives of animals around the world.

## WEBSITES

The internet is full of fascinating information about animals but unfortunately not all of it is true and you have to use discretion when it comes to which sources to believe. Here are a few recommendations.

**Wikipedia**  *http://en.wikipedia.org*

It's the online encyclopaedia that anyone can edit. That means that every so often you'll find something on Wikipedia that is inaccurate or sometimes just plain ridiculous, but the vast majority of editors who write and update the pages have both knowledge and integrity. So you'll need to use a little discretion but overall there is no better one-stop shop online for animal info.

**Tetrapod Zoology**  *http://scienceblogs.com/tetrapodzoology*

There are a lot of great bloggers out there writing about animal-related subjects. Darren Naish, who writes the superb 'Tet Zoo' blog, often explores the stranger side of animal life, concentrating on the four-limbed vertebrates both extant and extinct, and beautifully conveys his fascination with lively yet technically detailed posts. There are several other excellent natural history bloggers writing on scienceblogs.com – it's well worth having a browse around.

**EDGE of Existence**  *www.edgeofexistence.org*

EDGE is short for 'Evolutionarily Distinct and Globally

Endangered'. This website presents detailed biographies of some of the most remarkable species alive today, with details on the conservation efforts underway to preserve their unique contributions to Earth's biodiversity. It was launched by the Zoological Society of London in 2007; so far only mammals and amphibians are covered but other groups will be added in due course.

**Wild About Britain** *www.wildaboutbritain.co.uk*
This is a great big website covering all British wildlife. It includes photo galleries, a species-by-species encyclopaedia, book reviews and, perhaps best of all, very active message boards where you can talk about all the strange wildlife-relating goings-on you have observed lately.

**BBC Wildlife Magazine** *www.bbcwildlifemagazine.com*
The website for this massively popular publication contains news stories, articles, reviews and a members' forum.

### BOOKS

*Last Chance to See* by Douglas Adams and Mark Carwardine tells the tale of one zoologist and one over-awed comedy writer as they travel the world to see some of the rarest and most remarkable animals in existence.

*Life* by Martha Holmes and Michael Gunton is the book of the most recent David Attenborough BBC wildlife series. In words and stunning pictures it explores some of the most remarkable animal behaviour ever observed.

*Natural History Museum Animal Records* by Mark Carwardine brings together all of the biggest, smallest, fastest, slowest, highest, deepest, strongest and cleverest animals in one handy volume.

# OTHER NATURAL HISTORY TITLES
# FROM NEW HOLLAND

### Atlas of Rare Birds
*Dominic Couzens.* Amazing tales of 50 of the world's rarest birds, illustrated with a series of stunning photographs and colour maps. Endorsed by BirdLife International.
£24.99  ISBN 978 1 84773 693 2

### Chris Packham's Back Garden Nature Reserve
*Chris Packham.* A complete guide explaining the best ways to attract wildlife into your garden and to encourage it to stay there.
£12.99  ISBN 978 1 84773 698 7

### Colouring Birds
### Colouring Bugs
*Sally MacLarty.* Two ideal gifts to help develop a child's interest in wildlife. Each features 40 species outlines – including such favourites as Robin, Blue Tit, Red Admiral and Emperor Dragonfly – and a colour gallery depicting the birds or bugs as they would appear in life.
Each title: £2.99.  ISBNs: 978 184773 526 3 (Birds) and 978 184773 525 6 (Bugs)

### Common Garden Bird Calls
*Hannu Jännes and Owen Roberts.* Invaluable book and CD featuring the songs and calls of 60 species likely to be encountered in gardens and parks. Each is illustrated with at least one photo and a distribution map.
£6.99  ISBN 978 1 84773 517 1

**Creative Bird Photography**

*Bill Coster.* Illustrated with Bill Coster's inspirational images. An indispensable guide to all aspects of the subject, covering bird portraits, activities such as flight and courtship, and taking 'mood' shots at dawn and dusk.

£19.99  ISBN 978 1 84773 509 6


**The Garden Bird Year**

*Roy Beddard.* Gives both birdwatchers and gardeners insights into how to attract resident and migrant birds to the garden and how to manage this precious space as a vital resource for wildlife.

£9.99  ISBN 978 184773 503 4


**The History of Ornithology**

*Valerie Chansigaud.* The story of the development of a science that endlessly inspires us. Richly illustrated with numerous artworks, photographs and diagrams, including a detailed timeline of ornithological events.

£17.99  ISBN 978 1 84773 433 4


**The Naturalized Animals of Britain and Ireland**

*Christopher Lever.* Authoritative and eminently readable account of how alien species were introduced and naturalized, their status and distribution, and their impact. Includes everything from the Ruddy Duck to the Red-necked Wallaby.

£35.00  ISBN 978 1 84773 454 9

**New Holland Concise Bird Guide**
**New Holland Concise Butterfly & Moth Guide**
**New Holland Concise Wild Flower Guide**
Three ideal first field guides for children or adults that will fit
into even a small pocket. Each covers hundreds of species in
full colour, comes in a durable plastic wallet and includes a
fold-out insert comparing similar species.
Each title: £4.99. ISBN: 978 1 84773 601 7 (Birds), 978 1
84773 602 4 (Butterflies and Moths), 978 1 84773 603 1
(Wild Flowers)

**New Holland European Bird Guide**
*Peter H Barthel.* The only truly pocket-sized comprehensive
field guide to all the birds of Britain and Europe. Features more
than 1,700 beautiful and accurate artworks of more than 500
species.
£10.99  ISBN 978 1 84773 110 4

**Photographing Garden Wildlife**
*Marianne Taylor and Steve Young.* Even if your camera is a
simple compact, this book tells you all you need to know to
capture amazing wildlife shots in your own back yard.
£14.99  ISBN 978 1 84773 486 0

**Steve Backshall's Deadly 60**
*Steve Backshall.* As seen on BBC TV. Steve and his crew take a
round-the-world trip of a lifetime to seek out 60 of the world's
deadliest creatures, from tiny ticks to enormous elephants.
£9.99  ISBN 978 1 84773 430 3

## Steve Backshall's Wildlife Adventurer's Guide

*Steve Backshall.* Tips on everything from beachcombing, snorkelling and building your own hedgehog hotel to tree climbing, natural foods and how to make traps for insects and mammals.

£14.99  ISBN 978 1 84773 324 5


## Tales of a Tabloid Twitcher

*Stuart Winter.* The key ornithological events and personalities, scandal and gossip of the past two decades and beyond seen through the eyes of a birding journalist. A 'must-read' book for all birdwatchers.

£7.99  ISBN 978 1 84773 693 2


See *www.newhollandpublishers.com* for details and offers

I think I'll just
stay in here...